Better Homes and Gardens.

STEP·BY·STEP

Kids'

COOK BOOK

1984 by Meredith Corporation, Des Moines, Iowa.
All Rights Reserved. Printed in the United States of America.
First Edition. First Printing.
Library of Congress Card Catalog Number: 83-61317
ISBN: 0-696-01325-8

On the cover: Tasty Tacos (see recipe, page 66)

BETTER HOMES AND GARDENS® BOOKS

Editor: Gerald M. Knox
Art Director: Ernest Shelton
Managing Editor: David A. Kirchner

Food and Nutrition Editor: Nancy Byal
Department Head—Cook Books: Sharyl Heiken
Associate Department Heads: Sandra Granseth,
    Rosemary C. Hutchinson, Elizabeth Woolever
Senior Food Editors: Julie Henderson, Julia Malloy,
    Marcia Stanley
Associate Food Editors: Jill Burmeister,
    Molly Culbertson, Linda Foley, Linda Henry,
    Lynn Hoppe, Mary Jo Plutt, Maureen Powers,
    Joyce Trollope
Recipe Development Editor: Marion Viall
Test Kitchen Director: Sharon Stilwell
Test Kitchen Home Economists: Jean Brekke,
    Kay Cargill, Marilyn Cornelius, Maryellyn Krantz,
    Dianna Nolin, Marge Steenson

Associate Art Directors: Linda Ford Vermie,
    Neoma Alt West, Randall Yontz
Copy and Production Editors: Marsha Jahns,
    Mary Helen Schiltz, Carl Voss, David A. Walsh
Assistant Art Directors: Harijs Priekulis, Tom Wegner
Senior Graphic Designers: Alisann Dixon,
    Lynda Haupert, Lyne Neymeyer
Graphic Designers: Mike Burns, Mike Eagleton,
    Deb Miner, Stan Sams, D. Greg Thompson,
    Darla Whipple, Paul Zimmerman

Vice President, Editorial Director: Doris Eby
Group Editorial Services Director: Duane L. Gregg

General Manager: Fred Stines
Director of Publishing: Robert B. Nelson
Vice President, Retail Marketing: Jamie Martin
Vice President, Direct Marketing: Arthur Heydendael

STEP-BY-STEP KIDS' COOK BOOK

Editor: Linda Henry
Copy and Production Editor: David A. Walsh
Graphic Designer: Deb Miner
Electronic Text Processor: Jaquin I. Bodensteiner

Our seal assures you that every recipe in the **Step-By-Step Kids' Cook Book** has been tested in the Better Homes and Gardens® Test Kitchen. This means that each recipe is practical and reliable, and meets our high standards of taste appeal.

CONTENTS

Before you start making your favorite recipe, look over these cooking tips.

The success of any recipe you choose will depend on how accurate you are when you measure the ingredients. Learn how to measure correctly so *every* recipe turns out right *every* time!

Even beginning cooks can stir up good-tasting treats! You don't have to measure *or* cook any ingredients to enjoy *Salad-in-a-Pocket* or *Ice Cream Floats*.

There's a lot to learn when you first start cooking, such as stirring together a lot of different ingredients to make a batter, using a sharp knife to cut up vegetables, and handling all kinds of hot dishes. It's all part of becoming a good cook! You will learn these cooking skills in recipes such as *Apple Drop Biscuits* and *Oriental-Style Vegetables*.

Using kitchen appliances such as blenders and electric mixers can make cooking simpler! Testing cakes and breads to see if they're done is important, too. You can practice these skills by making *Easy Chocolate Cake* and *Gumdrop Nutbread*.

Spaghetti-Crust Pie and *Chunky Chocolate Cookies* combine skills you've learned. With more steps, they are longer recipes and may require more concentration.

HINTS FOR

Cooking is fun—a big adventure just waiting to happen! Your kitchen is like an undiscovered land, and you are its explorer! You know it's fun to eat lasagna, ice cream floats, and sticky, gooey cinnamon rolls, but did you know it's fun to make them, too? It's exciting to work with food and see how recipes turn out. You'll be so proud when you cook supper for your family or make snacks for your friends! And the food will seem to taste that much better just because *you* cooked it yourself.

This book starts out with very simple recipes. As you go through the book, the recipes become harder. With the help of how-to photographs in every recipe, you'll learn basic cooking steps. These steps are repeated and combined with more new steps as you go from easier to harder recipes. By the end of the book, you'll have learned and practiced many cooking basics.

Browse through the book to see which recipes you'd like to make. (You're sure to find lots!) Notice, too, that they may include variations and microwave instructions, when useful. This means you may be able to fix a favorite recipe more than one way, or use your microwave to speed things up.

Scattered throughout the book are some menu pages. Everything you'll need to know about putting the menus together is on these pages. Even the recipes appear with the menus, so you don't have to flip through the book to find them. Pay special attention to the menu timetables, which tell you when to do everything from putting the food into the oven to pouring the milk.

BEFORE YOU START TO COOK

Get into the habit of always doing a few things before you even begin to cook. First, roll up your sleeves and put on an apron so you keep your clothes clean. If you have long hair, pull it back so it doesn't get into the food. Then, wash your hands with soap and water, and dry them well.

READ THE RECIPE, THEN COLLECT EVERYTHING YOU NEED

Before preparing a recipe, read it thoroughly—all the way through. You want to make sure you know how to do everything and you have everything you need to fix the recipe. Get out all the equipment and ingredients listed.

Now, you may think you're ready to plunge into cooking, but hold off a bit longer. You have one more thing to do first—gather some help.

EVEN GREAT CHEFS NEED HELP!

When it comes to cooking, the greatest of chefs uses help to get things done. For you, it's a good idea to have not just any help, but adult help around when you're cooking. Your helper can answer questions, help you use kitchen tools, and help you with hot pans. Throughout the book, we have labeled recipe steps that may need adult help. Talk over these steps with your adult helper before you begin preparing the

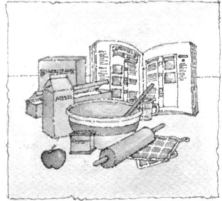

Read the recipe through and gather everything you need.

You may need some adult help.

Be careful when using the range top and oven.

recipe. Ask your adult helper to explain any words you don't understand. Older, more experienced chefs may not need as much adult help as younger or less experienced cooks!

Now you're ready to go! It's exciting to make a new recipe, but remember that safety comes first.

USING THE RANGE TOP AND OVEN

When you're cooking on top of the range, turn all the pan handles toward the middle so they don't stick out over the edge of the stove. Otherwise, someone could bump the pan and spill it when walking by. When you're stirring the food in a pan, hold the handle firmly. Stir with a wooden spoon or a metal spoon with a wooden or plastic handle. All-metal spoons can get hot enough to burn your fingers. Tilt the lid of a pan away from you as you take it off. This way the steam that comes rolling out can't burn you. And don't forget to turn the oven and range-top dials "off" when you've finished cooking.

WHAT ABOUT HOT PANS?

Always have hot pads handy, and make sure they're dry. Wet hot pads won't protect you from heat. Use hot pads whenever you take anything out of the oven or the broiler. When removing pans from the oven, use hot pads to pull out the oven rack a little way so you can lift out the pan more easily.

Be careful when you set a hot pan down. Make it a habit to always set the pan on a trivet, a wooden cutting board, or a cooling rack. Never set a hot pan directly on a table or counter top!

ALWAYS BE CAREFUL!

Sharp knives are dangerous! It's a good idea to check with your adult helper before you use a knife. Pick up a knife by its handle, not by the blade. When cutting, always use a cutting board and don't try to hold food in your hand when you cut it. Take care washing and drying your knives, too; keep the blade turned away from you. When you're not using them, store sharp knives in a place by themselves so you don't have to rummage through a drawer to find them.

When you plug in or disconnect an appliance, such as an electric mixer or can opener, be sure your hands are dry. Never pull the cord; instead, take hold of the plug and pull it straight out.

It's helpful to keep paper towels nearby to wipe up any spills. Clean up anything that spills on the floor right away so no one slips and falls.

REMEMBER—CLEAN UP!

Mom and Dad will be pleased if you leave the kitchen spotless! Cleaning up as you go makes the chore a lot easier. Put ingredients away as you finish with them, especially cold foods (such as milk, mayonnaise, or butter) that belong in the refrigerator. Be sure to put the lids on tight!

Dishes will be a lot easier to clean if you don't let the food dry on them first. Rinse them as soon as you're finished with them. And load the dishwasher if you're lucky enough to have one. Wash, dry, and put away all the equipment when you're finished cooking. Start by washing the least soiled items first, such as glasses and silverware, and end up with messy pots and pans.

Protect your hands and counter tops from hot pans.

Use knives and appliances with caution. Clean up spills right away.

Put things away as you use them. Rinse dishes before food dries.

HOW TO

LIQUIDS

Liquid measuring cups can be made of glass or clear plastic. They have pouring spouts that make it easy to pour the liquid out of the measuring cup without spilling it. These cups also have lines that mark certain measurements. You use liquid measuring cups to measure ingredients such as water, milk, and honey.

To correctly measure liquids, set the measuring cup on a flat surface. Bend down so your eyes are even with the measurement mark you need. (You will make mistakes if you hold the cup in your hand or read it from above the cup!) Add the liquid slowly till it reaches the mark you want.

Sometimes you have to do some simple math while you're cooking. For example, if you need 1½ cups of milk, fill a 1-cup measuring cup. Add the milk as the recipe says. Then fill the measuring cup to the ½-cup mark and add it to the recipe.

DRY INGREDIENTS

Single metal or plastic cups are used for measuring dry ingredients. To measure dry ingredients such as flour or sugar, use a dry measuring cup that's exactly the size you need. Pile the ingredient lightly into the measuring cup using a spoon, then level it off over waxed paper with the flat side of a narrow metal spatula or table knife.

When measuring flour, stir it slightly in the container before measuring. This makes it lighter and gives you the correct measure. Never dip a measuring cup into the flour as this will pack it.

Sometimes you'll need to use more than one measuring cup to get the amount you need. For example, if you need 1⅓ cups of flour, fill both the 1-cup dry measuring cup and the ⅓-cup dry measuring cup.

USING MEASURING SPOONS

Measuring spoons can be metal or plastic. Use the same set of measuring spoons for both liquid and dry ingredients. These are different from the spoons you use for eating, so be sure to pick the right size spoon.

For dry ingredients, fill the spoon, then level it off over waxed paper with the flat side of a narrow metal spatula or table knife. For liquid ingredients, simply fill the spoon to the top. (When you are filling a measuring spoon with any liquid, hold the spoon over the sink or over waxed paper, not over the mixing bowl with other ingredients. Then if it overflows a little bit, it won't go into your bowl.)

Recipes sometimes call for a dash of an ingredient, such as pepper. Just what does "dash" really mean? It's a measure of less than ⅛ teaspoon. Probably the best way to put a dash of pepper into a recipe is to just sprinkle a *little bit* out of a pepper shaker.

MEASURE

SHORTENING

To measure solid shortening, use a rubber scraper to scoop the shortening out of its container. Put the shortening into a dry measuring cup using the rubber scraper.

Push the shortening down into the measuring cup so you are measuring only shortening, not air. When the measuring cup is full, level off the top of the measuring cup with the flat side of a narrow metal spatula or a table knife.

To get the shortening out of the measuring cup, run the rubber scraper around the inside of the cup. Be sure to scrape out all the shortening—don't leave any in the measuring cup! You can measure peanut butter this same way.

BROWN SUGAR

Working over waxed paper, use a spoon to scoop brown sugar out of its container into a dry measuring cup. Use your hand to push the brown sugar into the measuring cup. Pack in the brown sugar till the cup is full and level.

To get the brown sugar out of the cup, run a narrow metal spatula or a table knife around the inside of the measuring cup. Turn the measuring cup upside down over your mixing bowl. If you've packed the brown sugar as firmly as possible, it should keep the shape of the measuring cup when you dump it out.

BUTTER OR MARGARINE

Sticks of butter or margarine are usually wrapped in foil or paper with measurements marked on the wrapper. This makes it easy for you to see how much to use.

Use 1 stick of butter or margarine when you need ½ cup. But if you need ¼ cup, ⅓ cup, or single tablespoons of butter or margarine, the markings on the wrapper will show you where to cut. Use a narrow metal spatula or a table knife to cut the butter or margarine.

If you're using the whole stick of butter or margarine, remove the wrapper and throw it away. But if you're using only part of the stick, remove the wrapper only from the part you will use. That way you'll have the wrapper on the rest of the stick to use as a guide the next time you need to measure butter.

SALAD-IN-A-POCKET

EQUIPMENT

kitchen scissors
paper towels
narrow metal
  spatula *or* table
  knife
mixing bowl

INGREDIENTS

2 large pita bread
  rounds
4 lettuce leaves
Mayonnaise,
  salad dressing,
  or prepared
  mustard
1 3-ounce package
  very thinly
  sliced ham
1 3-ounce package
  very thinly
  sliced chicken
  or turkey
4 ¾-ounce slices
  American *or*
  Swiss cheese
Sweet pickle
  slices

WASH HANDS

1 Use the kitchen scissors to cut the two pita bread rounds in half. Carefully open the bread with your fingers so you can see the pocket in the bread.

2 Rinse the lettuce leaves in cold water. Put the lettuce leaves onto paper towels to drain. Pat lettuce leaves dry with some more paper towels.

3 Using a narrow metal spatula or a table knife, spread some of the mayonnaise, the salad dressing, or the prepared mustard on the inside of the four pita bread pockets.

4 Use the kitchen scissors to cut open the packages of sliced ham and chicken or turkey. To make the sandwich filling, tear the ham, chicken or turkey, and American or Swiss cheese into bite-size pieces. Put the torn pieces into a mixing bowl. Add a few sweet pickle slices to the mixing bowl. Toss the filling together by using your hands to pick up and drop the mixture.

5 Put a lettuce leaf into each pita bread pocket. Stuff each pita bread pocket with some of the sandwich filling. Makes 4 pita sandwiches.

CLEAN UP

ICE CREAM FLOAT

EQUIPMENT

ice cream scoop
tall glass

INGREDIENTS

Vanilla ice
cream
Root beer *or* cola
soda pop

TRY IT THIS WAY

Rainbow Float:
Fill a tall glass *half*
full of cold *cranber-
ry juice cocktail.*
Carefully add 1
scoop of your favor-
ite *sherbet.* Slowly
fill the tall glass with
cold *lemon-lime
soda pop.* Makes
1 float.

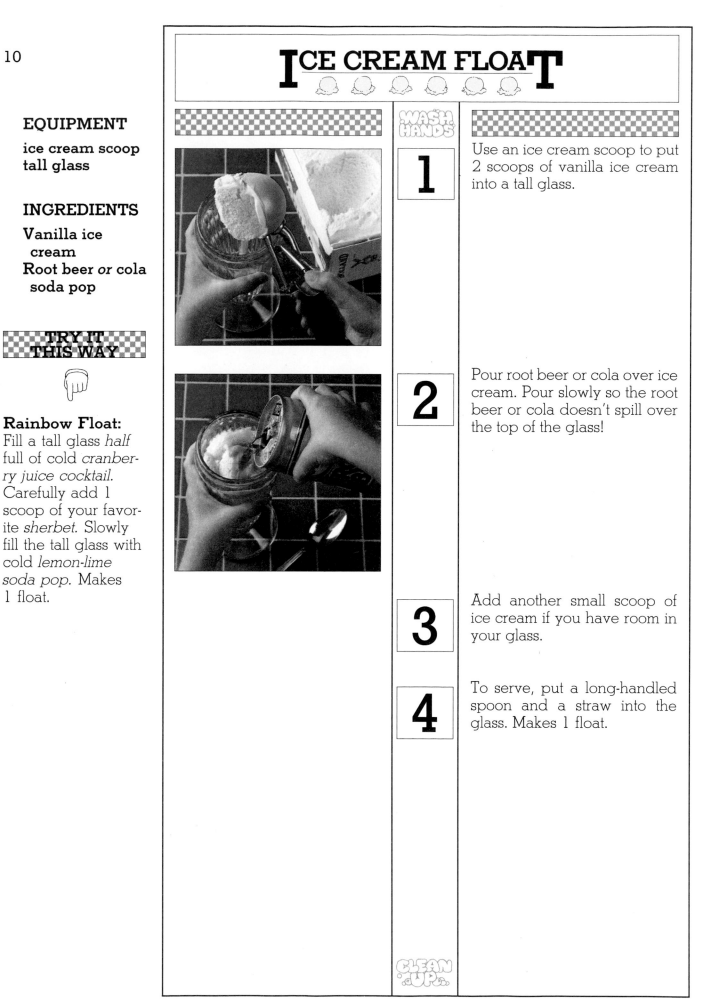

WASH HANDS

1 Use an ice cream scoop to put 2 scoops of vanilla ice cream into a tall glass.

2 Pour root beer or cola over ice cream. Pour slowly so the root beer or cola doesn't spill over the top of the glass!

3 Add another small scoop of ice cream if you have room in your glass.

4 To serve, put a long-handled spoon and a straw into the glass. Makes 1 float.

CLEAN UP

SUNNY DAY TEA

WASH HANDS

1

Fill the large jar with the cold water. Drape the tea bags over the lip of the jar so the tea bags are floating in the water and the strings are on the outside of the jar. Screw the lid onto jar so it holds strings in place.

2

Put the jar outside in the warm sunshine for 4 to 6 hours. Bring the jar inside and remove the tea bags. Squeeze all the water out of the tea bags. Throw tea bags away.

3

Serve the tea over ice cubes in tall glasses. Put one lemon wedge into each glass, if you like. Pass sugar, if you like. Keep any leftover tea in the refrigerator. Makes 6 servings.

EQUIPMENT

measuring cups
large jar with
  lid

INGREDIENTS

4 cups cold water
2 regular tea bags
  or herb-flavored
  tea bags
  Ice cubes
  Lemon wedges
  (if you like)
  Sugar
  (if you like)

Rainy Day Tea:
Follow the recipe for Sunny Day Tea, *but* let the jar stand in the refrigerator for 6 hours instead of standing in the sunshine.

CLEAN UP

ACCORDION SANDWICH LOAF

EQUIPMENT

oven
measuring cups
  and spoons
cutting board
bread knife
ruler
small mixing
  bowl
spoon
narrow metal
  spatula *or*
  table knife
foil
cookie sheet
hot pads

INGREDIENTS

1 loaf unsliced
  French bread
  (about 16 inches
  long)
¼ cup mayonnaise
  or salad
  dressing
2 teaspoons dried
  parsley flakes
2 teaspoons pre-
  pared mustard
½ teaspoon onion
  powder
8 ¾-ounce slices
  American *or*
  Swiss cheese
8 slices cooked
  ham

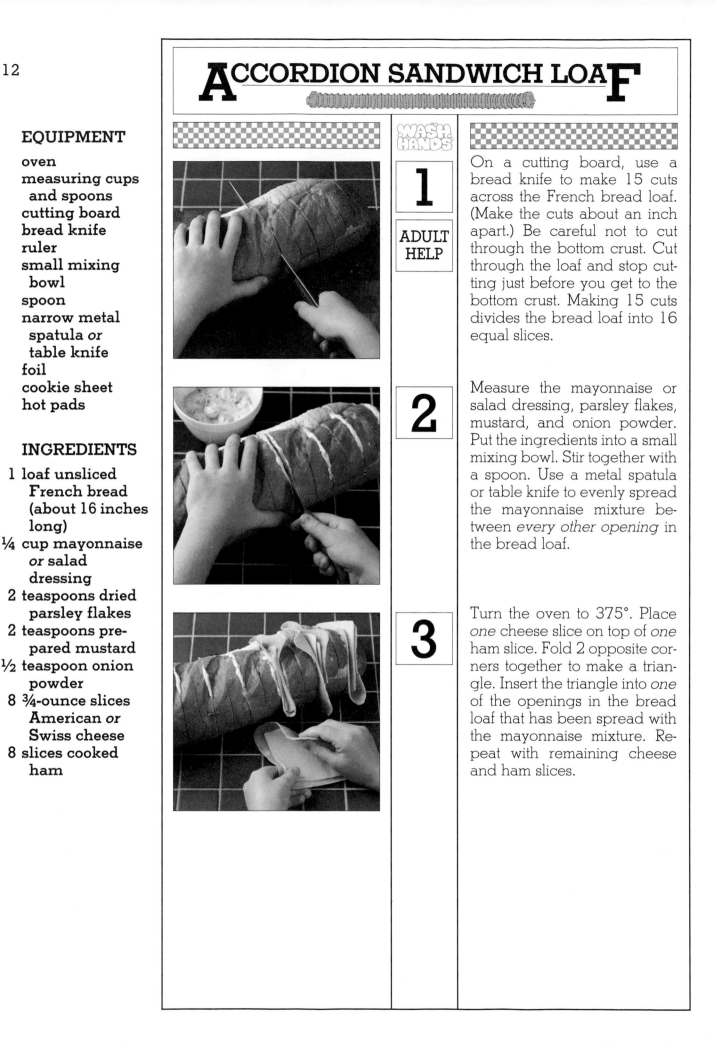

WASH HANDS

1 | **ADULT HELP**

On a cutting board, use a bread knife to make 15 cuts across the French bread loaf. (Make the cuts about an inch apart.) Be careful not to cut through the bottom crust. Cut through the loaf and stop cutting just before you get to the bottom crust. Making 15 cuts divides the bread loaf into 16 equal slices.

2

Measure the mayonnaise or salad dressing, parsley flakes, mustard, and onion powder. Put the ingredients into a small mixing bowl. Stir together with a spoon. Use a metal spatula or table knife to evenly spread the mayonnaise mixture between *every other opening* in the bread loaf.

3

Turn the oven to 375°. Place *one* cheese slice on top of *one* ham slice. Fold 2 opposite corners together to make a triangle. Insert the triangle into *one* of the openings in the bread loaf that has been spread with the mayonnaise mixture. Repeat with remaining cheese and ham slices.

Guaranteed to be as much of a hit with Mom and Dad
as it will be with you!

13

4

ADULT HELP

Press sandwich loaf together and wrap loaf in foil. Put loaf onto a cookie sheet and put it into the hot oven. Bake for 25 to 30 minutes or till hot. Turn off oven. Use hot pads to remove cookie sheet from oven. Use dry hot pads whenever you remove things from the oven. Wet hot pads do not protect you from the heat.

5

To serve the sandwich loaf, carefully remove the foil. Use the narrow metal spatula to cut through the bottom crusts of the *unfilled* openings in the bread loaf. This separates the loaf into 8 individual sandwiches. Makes 8 sandwiches.

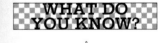

WHAT DO YOU KNOW?

A bread knife has a long, narrow blade that's especially good for slicing fresh bread. The sharp edge on the blade of a bread knife is not straight, but is "serrated," which means it has sawlike notches that gently tear the bread instead of cutting it. When you slice fresh bread, use a gentle "sawing" action so you don't crush the bread.

APPLE DROP BISCUITS

EQUIPMENT

oven
measuring cups
  and spoons
medium mixing
  bowl
plastic bag
rolling pin
wooden spoon
vegetable peeler
waxed paper
shredder
cookie sheet
paper towel
large spoon
small spoon
ruler
hot pads
pancake turner

INGREDIENTS

2 cups packaged
  biscuit mix
2 tablespoons
  sugar
½ teaspoon ground
  cinnamon
¼ teaspoon ground
  nutmeg
½ cup walnut
  pieces
1 small apple
½ cup apple cider,
  apple juice, *or*
  milk
Shortening

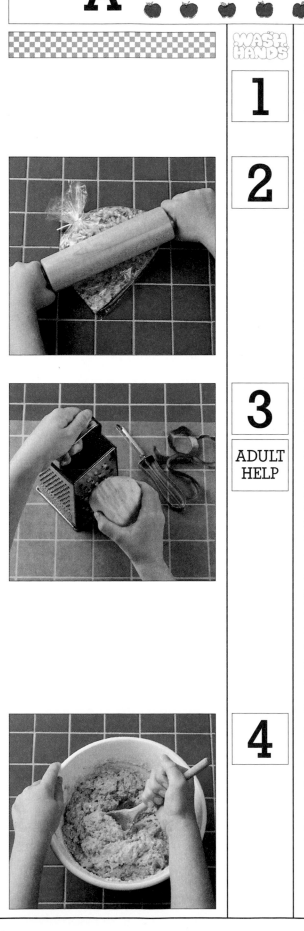

WASH HANDS

1 Measure the biscuit mix, sugar, cinnamon, and nutmeg. Put into a medium mixing bowl.

2 Measure the walnut pieces. Put the walnut pieces into a plastic bag. Close bag. Use a rolling pin to crush the nuts. Put the crushed nuts into the mixing bowl with the biscuit mix. Stir with a wooden spoon.

3 **ADULT HELP** Rinse the apple in cold water. Use a vegetable peeler to remove the skin from the apple. Throw the skin away. Put a sheet of waxed paper under the shredder to catch the apple as you shred it. Hold the shredder with one hand and move the apple down across it to cut into long, thin pieces. As you shred, keep turning the apple around to shred it on all sides. Watch your fingers and knuckles! Stop shredding the apple when you get to the core. Throw the core and the seeds away. Put the shredded apple into the mixing bowl.

4 Turn the oven to 450°. Measure apple cider, apple juice, or milk. Pour into mixing bowl with the biscuit mix, nuts, and shredded apple. Stir with the wooden spoon till dry ingredients are wet. Batter should be lumpy, so do not stir too much.

5

Grease the cookie sheet by putting a little bit of shortening on a folded paper towel. Spread the shortening evenly over the cookie sheet.

6

To drop biscuit dough onto the cookie sheet, get enough of the dough on a large spoon so dough is slightly humped in the spoon. With the back of a small spoon, push dough onto the cookie sheet. Leave about 2 inches between biscuits.

7

ADULT HELP

Put the cookie sheet into the hot oven. Bake for 10 to 12 minutes or till the biscuits are golden. Turn off the oven. Use hot pads to remove the cookie sheet from the oven. Use a pancake turner to remove the biscuits from the cookie sheet. Serve the hot biscuits immediately. Makes about 12 biscuits.

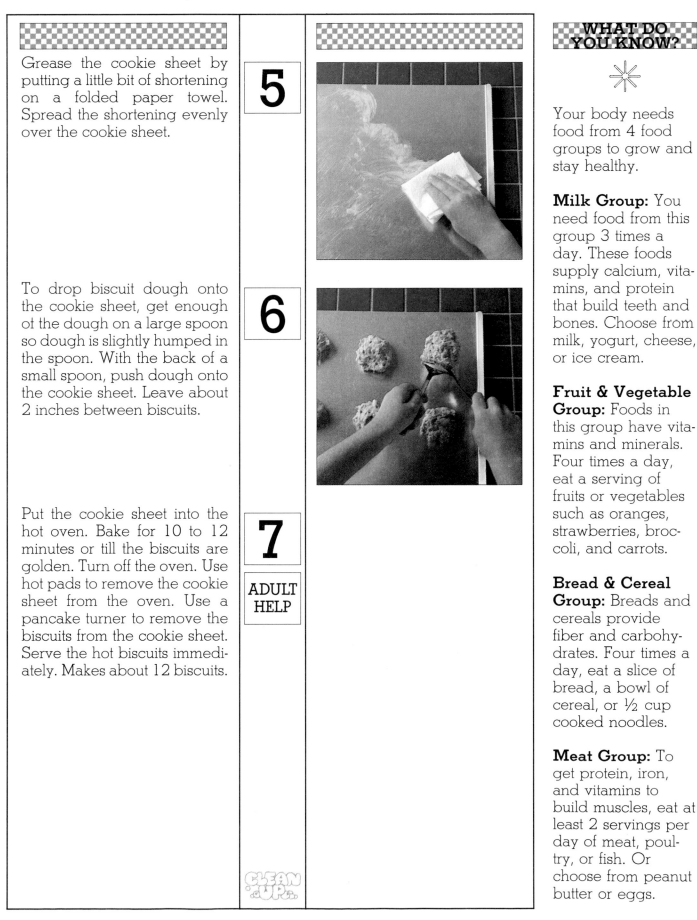

WHAT DO YOU KNOW?

Your body needs food from 4 food groups to grow and stay healthy.

Milk Group: You need food from this group 3 times a day. These foods supply calcium, vitamins, and protein that build teeth and bones. Choose from milk, yogurt, cheese, or ice cream.

Fruit & Vegetable Group: Foods in this group have vitamins and minerals. Four times a day, eat a serving of fruits or vegetables such as oranges, strawberries, broccoli, and carrots.

Bread & Cereal Group: Breads and cereals provide fiber and carbohydrates. Four times a day, eat a slice of bread, a bowl of cereal, or ½ cup cooked noodles.

Meat Group: To get protein, iron, and vitamins to build muscles, eat at least 2 servings per day of meat, poultry, or fish. Or choose from peanut butter or eggs.

SUNSHINE LEMONADE

EQUIPMENT

measuring cups
cutting board
sharp knife
citrus juicer
pitcher
large spoon

INGREDIENTS

5 lemons
4 cups water
¾ cup sugar
Ice cubes
Lemon slices
   (if you like)
Strawberries
   (if you like)

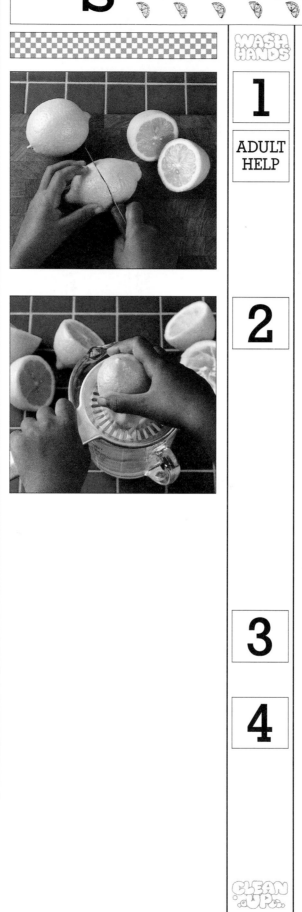

WASH HANDS

1

ADULT HELP

On a cutting board, use a sharp knife to cut each lemon in half through the middle. Hold each lemon tightly while you cut it so it doesn't roll around. Whenever you are cutting with a knife, use a cutting board so you don't cut the counter top.

2

Hold a citrus juicer on the top of a 2-cup measuring cup. Squeeze the juice from a lemon half by turning it back and forth on the citrus juicer till all the juice is out. Push down hard as you turn so you get all the juice out of the lemon half and into the measuring cup. Throw away the lemon pulp and seeds that gather in the juicer. Repeat with remaining lemon halves. After squeezing the lemon halves, you should have about 1 cup lemon juice. Pour the lemon juice into a pitcher.

3

Measure the water and the sugar. Add them to the pitcher with the lemon juice.

4

Use a large spoon to stir together all the ingredients in the pitcher. Stir till the sugar dissolves. Pour the lemonade over ice cubes in tall glasses. Put a lemon slice and a strawberry into each glass, if you like. Makes 6 or 7 servings.

CLEAN UP

TRY IT THIS WAY 👇

Orange Lemonade:
Follow the recipe for
Sunshine Lemonade,
but use the juice from
two oranges and
three lemons and use
only ½ cup sugar.

HOT TAMALE BAKE

EQUIPMENT

oven
measuring cups
can opener
cutting board
sharp knife
rubber scraper
1½-quart
  casserole
foil
plastic bag
rolling pin
kitchen scissors
hot pads

INGREDIENTS

1 15-ounce can
  tamales
4 hot dogs
1 15-ounce can
  chili without
  beans
1 8-ounce can
  tomato sauce
2 cups corn chips
½ of a 4-ounce
  package (½ cup)
  shredded ched-
  dar cheese
  Dairy sour cream
  (if you like)
  Pitted black
  olives
  (if you like)

WASH HANDS

1

ADULT HELP

Use a can opener to open the can of tamales. Remove any paper that may be wrapped around the tamales. On a cutting board, use a sharp knife to cut across each tamale so you have 3 equal-size pieces. Then cut across each hot dog so you have 4 equal-size pieces.

2

ADULT HELP

Turn the oven to 350°. Open the can of chili without beans and the can of tomato sauce. Use a rubber scraper to empty the cans into a 1½-quart casserole. Add the cut-up hot dogs. Stir with the rubber scraper till well mixed. Top casserole with the cut-up tamales. Cover the casserole with a lid or foil. Put casserole into the oven. Bake for 35 minutes.

While the casserole is baking, measure the corn chips. Put half of the corn chips at a time into a plastic bag. Close bag. Use a rolling pin to crush the corn chips. Set the crushed corn chips aside till you are ready to use them. Use kitchen scissors to cut open the package of cheese. Remove *half* of the cheese from the package and set the cheese aside till you're ready to use it.

Use hot pads to remove the casserole from the oven. Use hot pads to remove the lid or foil. (Be careful because steam can burn you when you remove the lid or the foil.) Sprinkle the crushed corn chips around the edge of the casserole. Sprinkle the shredded cheddar cheese in the center of the casserole.

Use hot pads to put the casserole back into the hot oven. Do not cover. Bake 10 minutes more. Turn off the oven. Use hot pads to remove casserole from oven. Serve with a large spoon. Top each serving with sour cream and black olives, if you like. Makes 4 servings.

3

4

ADULT HELP

5

ADULT HELP

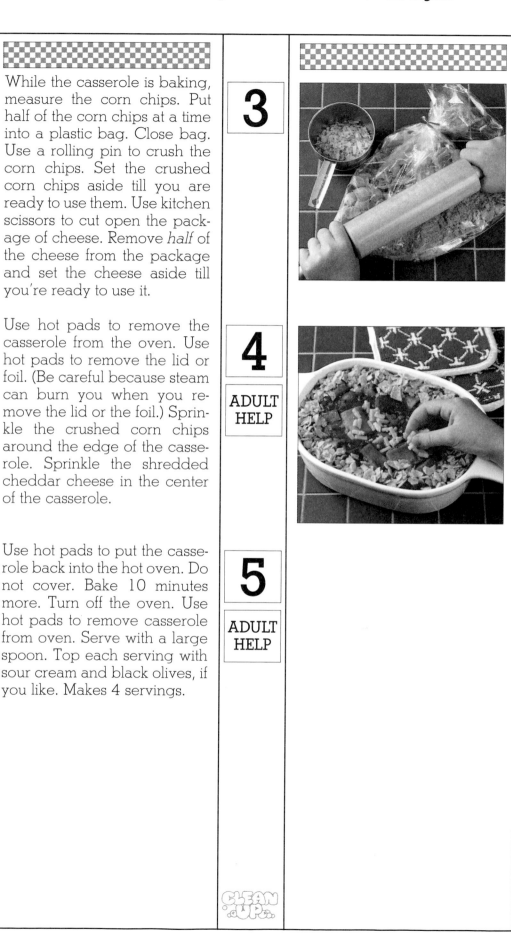

WHAT DO YOU KNOW?

It's important that every good cook know how to set a table.

The silverware and dinner plate go 1 inch from the edge of the table. The knife and spoon go on the right side of the plate, with the knife closest to the plate. The blade of the knife turns toward the plate because that way it's ready to be picked up. The fork goes on the left side of the plate.

A glass for milk or water belongs on the right side (at the tip of the knife) because most people pick it up with their right hand.

If you have a salad plate, it's placed at the tip of the fork. Napkins go to the left of the fork. If you like, you can put each napkin on a dinner plate.

CLEAN UP

NIFTY NACHOS

EQUIPMENT

oven
waxed paper
shredder
15x10x1-inch
  baking pan
  or 12-inch
  pizza pan
hot pads

INGREDIENTS

6 ounces cheddar
  cheese (1½ cups
  shredded)
Plain tortilla
  chips
Taco sauce
  (if you like)

WASH HANDS

1 ADULT HELP

Turn the oven to 400°. Put a sheet of waxed paper under the shredder to catch the cheese as you shred it. Hold the shredder with one hand and move the cheese down across the shredder to cut it into long, thin pieces. Be careful not to get your fingers or knuckles too close.

2 ADULT HELP

Spread tortilla chips in a single layer in the 15x10x1-inch baking pan or 12-inch pizza pan (you'll need about 30 chips). Sprinkle the shredded cheddar cheese over the chips. Put the baking or pizza pan into the hot oven. Bake for 2 to 3 minutes or till cheese melts. Turn off oven. Use hot pads to remove pan from oven.

3

Dip nachos into taco sauce as you eat them, if you like them spicy hot. Makes about 30.

CLEAN UP

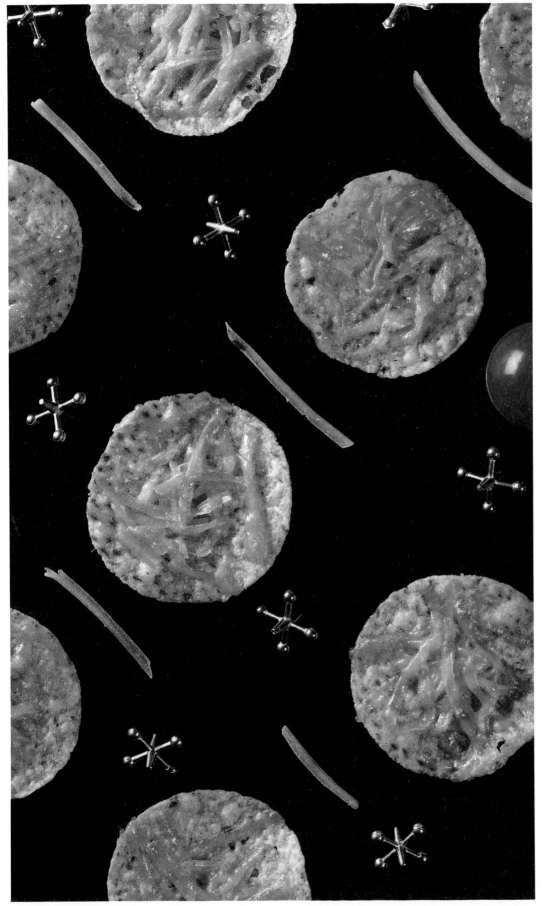

Fancy Nachos:
Follow the recipe
for Nifty Nachos,
but try sprinkling
chopped, pitted
black olives,
chopped *green
olives, or cooked
bacon pieces* on top
of the shredded
cheese before you
put the tortilla chips
into the oven.

For super-fast and
easy nachos, use
packages of shred-
ded cheese instead
of taking the time to
shred your own.
Store any extra
shredded cheese in
the refrigerator so
the next time you
get a craving for na-
chos, the cheese is
ready to go!

ZOO CAGE SALADS

Zoo Cages

On a cutting board, use a sharp knife to cut the end of 1 large *orange*. Throw away end slices. Cut rest of orange into ½-inch-thick slices. (Cut another large *orange* the same way, if you need more cages.) For each cage, put 1 orange slice on a plate. Use your fingers to tear a little *parsley*. Fill center of orange slice with parsley. Put *Owl, Monster,* or *Mouse Salad* on parsley. Poke wooden picks into edge of orange slice. Put another orange slice on top of picks for roof of cage.

ADULT HELP

Owl Salad

On a cutting board, use a table knife to cut a 1½-inch piece of *banana*. With the table knife, spread *soft-style cream cheese* over banana. Put 3 or 4 *rich round crackers* into a plastic bag. Close bag. Use a rolling pin to crush crackers. Roll banana in crushed crackers. To make eyes, use sharp knife to cut 2 thin *carrot slices*. Put a dab of cream cheese in center of each carrot slice. Push a *currant or raisin* into the cream cheese. Use a whole *almond* for a nose. Attach eyes and nose with more cream cheese.

ADULT HELP

Monster Salad

On a cutting board, use a table knife to cut a 1½-inch piece of *banana*. With the table knife, spread *soft-style cream cheese* over banana. Roll banana in *colored coconut or shredded carrot*. To color the coconut, put a little *coconut* into a plastic bag. Add 1 or 2 drops of your favorite *food coloring* to plastic bag. Close bag and shake it to color coconut. To shred the carrot, put a sheet of waxed paper under a shredder to catch the carrot as you shred it. Hold shredder with 1 hand and move 1 small *carrot* down across the shredder to cut it into long, thin pieces. Use *currants, raisins, or miniature semisweet chocolate pieces* for the eyes. Attach eyes to the banana with cream cheese.

Mouse Salad

On a cutting board, use a table knife to cut a 1½-inch piece of *banana*. Use a pastry brush to brush banana with a little *lemon juice.* Let the banana piece stand till dry. Press 2 sliced *almonds* into the top of the banana piece for ears. Use *raisins or miniature semisweet chocolate pieces* for the eyes. Use a *whole almond or peanut* for a nose. Attach the eyes and nose to the banana with *soft-style cream cheese.* Break 1 piece of uncooked *spaghetti* into 6 smaller pieces. Push the spaghetti pieces into the banana around the nose for whiskers. Push a piece of *black shoestring licorice* into the back of the banana for a tail, if you like.

ADULT HELP

TIC-TAC-TOE TOSTADAS

EQUIPMENT

oven
measuring cups
 and spoons
paper towel
cutting board
sharp knife
can opener
rubber scraper
small mixing
 bowl
15x10x1-inch
 baking pan
spoon
hot pads
pancake turner

INGREDIENTS

1 small green
 pepper
9 pitted black
 olives
4 ¾-ounce slices
 American
 cheese
1 15-ounce can
 chili with beans
1 teaspoon minced
 dried onion
6 packaged
 tostada shells

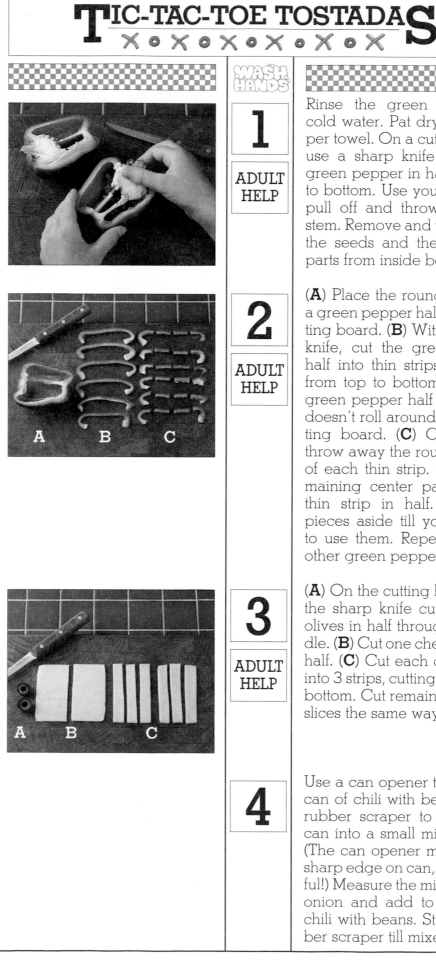

WASH HANDS

1 ADULT HELP

Rinse the green pepper in cold water. Pat dry with a paper towel. On a cutting board, use a sharp knife to cut the green pepper in half from top to bottom. Use your fingers to pull off and throw away the stem. Remove and throw away the seeds and the soft white parts from inside both halves.

2 ADULT HELP

(**A**) Place the rounded side of a green pepper half on the cutting board. (**B**) With the sharp knife, cut the green pepper half into thin strips, cutting it from top to bottom. Hold the green pepper half tightly so it doesn't roll around on the cutting board. (**C**) Cut off and throw away the rounded ends of each thin strip. Cut the remaining center part of each thin strip in half. Set these pieces aside till you're ready to use them. Repeat with the other green pepper half.

3 ADULT HELP

(**A**) On the cutting board, with the sharp knife cut the black olives in half through the middle. (**B**) Cut one cheese slice in half. (**C**) Cut each cheese half into 3 strips, cutting from top to bottom. Cut remaining cheese slices the same way.

4

Use a can opener to open the can of chili with beans. Use a rubber scraper to empty the can into a small mixing bowl. (The can opener may leave a sharp edge on can, so be careful!) Measure the minced dried onion and add to bowl with chili with beans. Stir with rubber scraper till mixed well.

Playing with your food is impolite, but your folks won't care if you play a game of tic-tac-toe on these tostadas!

25

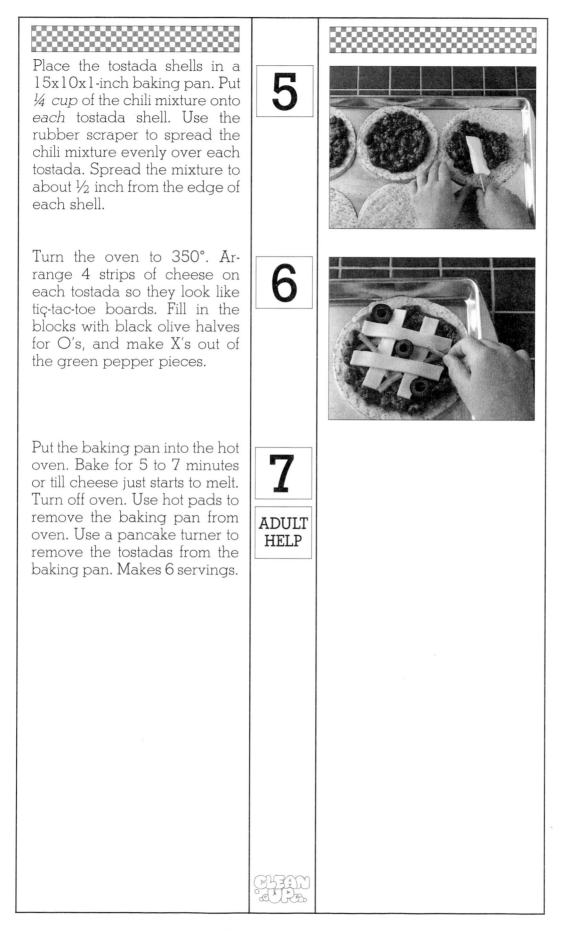

5

Place the tostada shells in a 15x10x1-inch baking pan. Put *¼ cup* of the chili mixture onto *each* tostada shell. Use the rubber scraper to spread the chili mixture evenly over each tostada. Spread the mixture to about ½ inch from the edge of each shell.

6

Turn the oven to 350°. Arrange 4 strips of cheese on each tostada so they look like tic-tac-toe boards. Fill in the blocks with black olive halves for O's, and make X's out of the green pepper pieces.

7

ADULT HELP

Put the baking pan into the hot oven. Bake for 5 to 7 minutes or till cheese just starts to melt. Turn off oven. Use hot pads to remove the baking pan from oven. Use a pancake turner to remove the tostadas from the baking pan. Makes 6 servings.

CLEAN UP

ORIENTAL-STYLE VEGETABLES

EQUIPMENT

range top
measuring cups
   and spoons
waxed paper
vegetable peeler
cutting board
sharp knife
2-quart saucepan
   with lid
small spoon
fork
colander

INGREDIENTS

2 medium carrots
1¼ cups water
1 tablespoon soy
   sauce
1 teaspoon sugar
½ teaspoon lemon
   juice
   Dash ground
   ginger
1 6-ounce package
   frozen pea pods

WASH HANDS

1 ADULT HELP

Rinse the carrots in cold water. Working over waxed paper, use a vegetable peeler to scrape the skin off a carrot. Scrape from one end to the other, always scraping away from you. Keep turning the carrot around, scraping on all sides. Repeat with the second carrot. Throw the carrot peelings away.

2 ADULT HELP

On a cutting board, use a sharp knife to cut the ends off the peeled carrots. Throw the end slices away. Bias-slice the peeled carrots into thin slices. To bias-slice, hold the knife at an angle while you cut the carrots. (Vegetables sliced this way have a greater cut surface, so they cook quickly.) Put carrot slices into the saucepan.

3 ADULT HELP

Measure water. Pour the water into the pan with carrots. Put the pan onto the burner. Turn burner to high heat. When the water starts to boil, turn the burner to medium-high heat. Cover the pan with the lid. Cook carrots for 6 minutes.

4

While the carrots are cooking, measure the soy sauce, sugar, lemon juice, and ginger. Put into a liquid measuring cup. Use a small spoon to stir till well mixed.

5 ADULT HELP

Uncover the saucepan. Carefully add the frozen pea pods. Cover the saucepan and cook about 4 minutes more. To see if the vegetables are done, poke them with a fork. They should feel tender, but still slightly crisp.

Eating these vegetables is a fun challenge if you use chopsticks, not silverware!

6 ADULT HELP

Turn burner off. Take pan off burner. To drain the vegetables, place a colander in the sink. Pour the vegetables and cooking liquid from saucepan into colander. Be careful of the steam as you pour vegetables out of the pan. Let the vegetables stand a few minutes to drain. Put drained vegetables into a serving bowl.

7 CLEAN UP

Use the spoon to stir the soy sauce mixture in the measuring cup. Pour the soy sauce mixture over carrots and pea pods. Stir soy sauce mixture into vegetables, coating them well. Makes 4 or 5 servings.

WHAT DO YOU KNOW?

To make eating these vegetables really fun, give everyone chopsticks instead of a fork! (You can buy them at most kitchen supply stores.) Try to use the chopsticks correctly (by holding them in the same hand), or put one chopstick in each hand and pick up the vegetables any way you can!

Spreadable Sandwiches

ADULT HELP

Chunky Carrot Sandwiches

Shred 1 small *carrot*. To shred, put a sheet of waxed paper under a shredder to catch the carrot as you shred it. Hold the shredder with one hand and move the carrot down across the shredder to cut it into long, thin pieces. Put the shredded carrot into a small bowl.

For the sandwich filling, measure ⅓ cup *chunk-style peanut butter* and 1 tablespoon *orange marmalade*. Add to the small bowl with the shredded carrot. Use a spoon to stir till mixed well.

For one sandwich, use a narrow metal spatula to spread one slice of *raisin bread* with *half* of the carrot mixture. Put another slice of *raisin bread* on top of the carrot mixture. Make another sandwich the same way. Makes 2 sandwiches.

Tropical Sandwiches

Measure ⅓ cup *creamy peanut butter*. Put the peanut butter into a small bowl. Measure 1 tablespoon *coconut* and 1 tablespoon drained *crushed pineapple*. Add coconut and pineapple to bowl with peanut butter. Use a spoon to stir till mixed well.

For one sandwich, use a narrow metal spatula to spread one slice of *bread* with *half* of the peanut butter mixture. Put another slice of *bread* on top of peanut butter mixture. Make another sandwich the same way. Makes 2 sandwiches.

Creamy Nut Sandwiches

Put half an 8-ounce container *soft-style cream cheese* into
a small bowl. Measure 2 tablespoons *mayonnaise or salad
dressing*. Put mayonnaise or
salad dressing into the bowl
with the cream cheese.

Measure 2 tablespoons *peanuts*. Put peanuts into a plastic
bag. Close bag. Use a rolling
pin to crush peanuts. Put the
crushed peanuts into the bowl
with the cream cheese and
mayonnaise mixture. Use a
spoon to stir till mixed well.

For one sandwich, use a narrow metal spatula to spread
one slice of *whole wheat
bread* with *half* of the peanut
mixture. Put another slice of
whole wheat bread on top of
the peanut mixture. Make another sandwich the same way.
Makes 2 sandwiches.

Creamy Raisin Sandwiches:
Follow the recipe for *Creamy
Nut Sandwiches, but* stir 2 tablespoons *light or dark raisins*
into cream cheese and mayonnaise instead of peanuts.

Cream Cheese and Apple Butter Sandwich

For one sandwich, use a narrow metal spatula to spread
one slice of *raisin bread* with a
little *soft-style cream cheese.*
Spread 1 tablespoon *apple
butter* on top of the cream
cheese. Put another slice of *raisin bread* on top of the apple
butter. If you like, make more
sandwiches the same way.

MINI MEAT MOUNDS

EQUIPMENT

oven
measuring cups
  and spoons
plastic bag
rolling pin
large mixing
  bowl
fork
wooden spoon
waxed paper
13x9x2-inch
  baking pan
hot pads
spoon
pancake turner

INGREDIENTS

8 saltine crackers
1 egg
¼ cup milk
1 teaspoon minced
  dried onion
1 pound lean
  ground beef
12 dill pickle slices
⅓ cup chili sauce

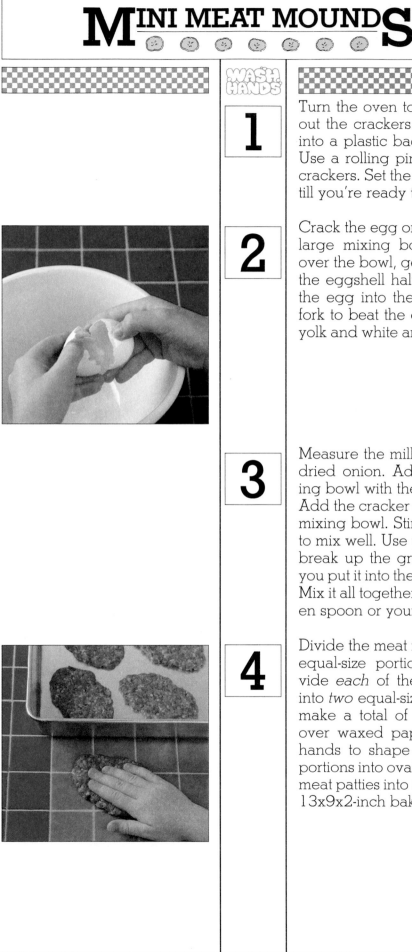

WASH HANDS

1 Turn the oven to 350°. Count out the crackers. Put crackers into a plastic bag. Close bag. Use a rolling pin to crush the crackers. Set the crumbs aside till you're ready to use them.

2 Crack the egg on the side of a large mixing bowl. Working over the bowl, gently separate the eggshell halves and pour the egg into the bowl. Use a fork to beat the egg lightly till yolk and white are mixed well.

3 Measure the milk and minced dried onion. Add to the mixing bowl with the beaten egg. Add the cracker crumbs to the mixing bowl. Stir with the fork to mix well. Use your hands to break up the ground beef as you put it into the mixing bowl. Mix it all together with a wooden spoon or your hands.

4 Divide the meat mixture into 6 equal-size portions. Then divide *each* of the six portions into *two* equal-size portions, to make a total of 12. Working over waxed paper, use your hands to shape the 12 meat portions into oval patties. Put *6* meat patties into an ungreased 13x9x2-inch baking pan.

You're in for a surprise when you get to the center of these
miniature meat loaves!

31

5

Press *2* dill pickle slices into the middle of *each* meat patty in the baking pan. Put another meat patty on top of each patty in the baking pan. Press the meat down around the pickles to seal the edges.

6

ADULT HELP

Put the baking pan into the hot oven. Bake for 25 minutes. While the mini meat mounds are baking, measure the chili sauce.

7

ADULT HELP

Use hot pads to remove the pan from the oven. Spoon a little bit of the chili sauce on top of each mini meat mound.

8

ADULT HELP

Use hot pads to put the pan back into the hot oven. Bake for 10 minutes more. Turn off oven. Use hot pads to remove the pan from the oven. Use a pancake turner to remove the mini meat mounds from the baking pan. Makes 6 servings.

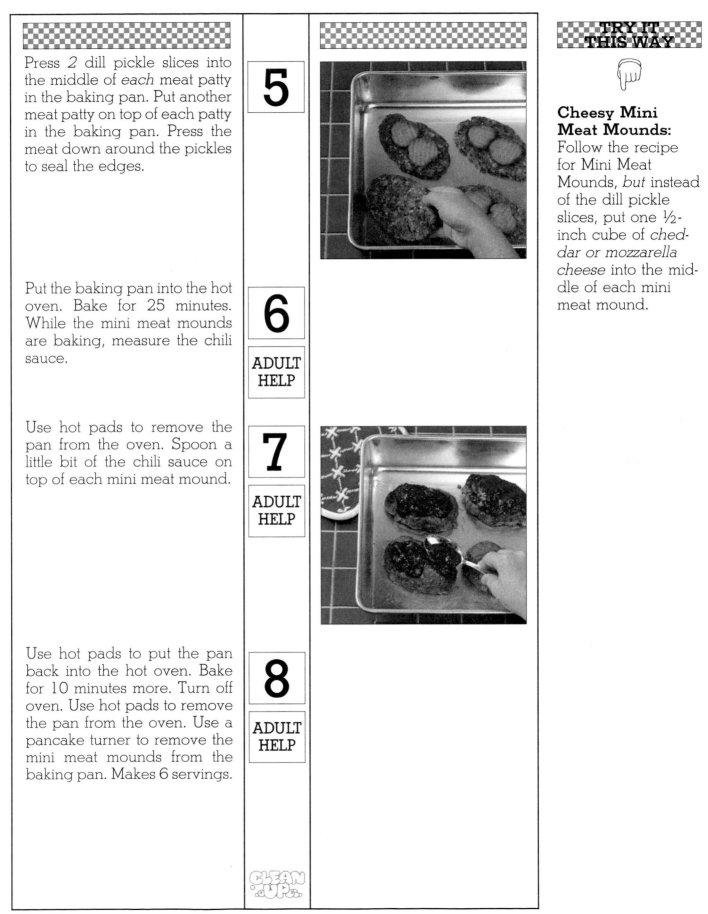

TRY IT THIS WAY

Cheesy Mini Meat Mounds: Follow the recipe for Mini Meat Mounds, *but* instead of the dill pickle slices, put one ½-inch cube of *cheddar or mozzarella cheese* into the middle of each mini meat mound.

MENU
GOOD-MORNING BREAKFAST

Scrambled Eggs
from a Jar

Canadian-Style Bacon

English muffins

Chocolate milk or
orange juice

Ever wonder where the word "breakfast" came from? It is really a combination of two different words: "break" and "fast." "Fast" means "to not eat." So when you sit down to eat the first meal of the day, you are really "breaking a fast."

Some weekend morning, let your parents be lazybones. You be the early bird and make breakfast for your family!

Before you begin, read through both of these pages to make sure you understand everything. Check the ingredient and equipment lists to be sure you have everything you need. (This menu will feed four people.)

When setting the table, you'll need a plate, a mug or glass, fork, knife, spoon, and napkin for each person. And don't forget to put your favorite jam on the table for the English muffins.

When breakfast is over, wash all the dishes and clean up the kitchen. If you clean up as you cook, this won't take long at all. Don't be surprised if Mom and Dad ask for another breakfast like this one soon!

Get Ready for Breakfast

- **35 minutes before serving:** Set the table.

- **30 minutes before serving:** Split 4 English muffins and put them into a toaster. Toast till golden brown. Butter the hot muffin halves and put them onto a plate. Cover the plate with foil so the muffins stay warm.

- **20 minutes before serving:** To cook the Canadian-Style Bacon, use kitchen scissors to cut open a package of presliced Canadian-style bacon. Remove 8 slices of bacon from the package. Put bacon slices into a 10-inch skillet. Put skillet onto burner. Turn burner to medium-low heat.

  After the bacon starts to sizzle, cook for 2 minutes on the first side. Use tongs to turn the bacon slices over. Cook about 2 minutes on the second side or till the edges of the bacon slices are lightly browned. Turn off burner.

  Use tongs to remove the bacon from the skillet. Place bacon on a serving platter. Cover the platter with foil to keep bacon warm. (You can cook the scrambled eggs in this same skillet.)

- **10 minutes before serving:** Prepare the **SCRAMBLED EGGS FROM A JAR.** Follow the recipe directions at right. Remove cooked eggs from the skillet. Place eggs on the platter with the cooked bacon.

- **At serving time:** Pour chocolate milk or orange juice. Remove the foil from the plate with the muffin halves. Place the food on the table, and you're ready to eat breakfast!

SCRAMBLED EGGS FROM A JAR

EQUIPMENT	INGREDIENTS
range top	8 eggs
measuring cups and spoons	¼ cup milk
small bowl	½ teaspoon salt (if you like)
1-quart wide-mouth jar with lid	Dash pepper
10-inch skillet	1 tablespoon butter *or* margarine
wooden spoon	

 1 Crack *one* of the eggs on the side of a small bowl. Working over the bowl, gently separate the eggshell halves over the bowl and pour the egg into the bowl. Put the egg into the 1-quart wide-mouth jar. Repeat with the remaining 7 eggs.

 2 Measure the milk, salt (if you want to add it), and pepper. Add to the jar with the eggs. Screw the lid onto the jar tightly. Shake the jar till the ingredients are mixed well.

 3 ADULT HELP Measure the butter or margarine. Put the butter or margarine into a 10-inch skillet. Put skillet onto burner. Turn burner to medium heat. When butter or margarine bubbles, pour the egg mixture out of the jar and into the skillet with the melted butter or margarine. Cook for 1 minute without stirring.

 **4 ADULT HELP** Use a wooden spoon to stir the eggs gently. (Do not stir too much or the eggs will be mushy.) Continue cooking over medium heat, stirring often, about 4 minutes or till the eggs are cooked but still moist looking. Turn off burner. Remove skillet from burner. Serve eggs right away. Makes 4 servings.

Cheesy Eggs: Follow the recipe for *Scrambled Eggs from a Jar, but* add ¼ cup shredded *cheddar cheese* to the jar with the egg mixture before shaking it up. The cheese melts as you cook the eggs.

Bacon and Eggs: Follow the recipe for *Scrambled Eggs from a Jar, but* add 1 tablespoon *cooked bacon pieces* to the jar with the egg mixture before shaking it up.

MENU
HOBO PICNIC

Banana Dogs

Pickle Pops

Apples

Cookies

Canned fruit juice
or lemonade

Picnics are always fun! It doesn't matter whether you go to a city park or your own backyard. You can spread a blanket under a shade tree or set up lawn chairs on a patio.

Wherever you decide to go for your picnic, why not carry the food hobo style? Pack your picnic lunch (except for the drink) in a large bandanna. Tie the bandanna to a big stick or old broom handle and carry it over your shoulder. When you get to your picnic spot, untie the bandanna and it will become your tablecloth!

Before leaving home, pack the fruit juice or lemonade in a picnic basket. Put paper plates and napkins in the picnic basket, too. They will save on the dishwashing when you get home. And don't forget to pack plastic or paper cups for your fruit juice or lemonade.

Because picnics are sometimes a spur-of-the-moment idea, you might want to take a shortcut and prepare frozen lemonade instead of squeezing lemons for fresh lemonade. You can also choose your favorite kind of packaged cookies, if you don't have homemade cookies.

Remember to throw any garbage into trash containers when you're ready to leave. Don't litter any public parks or your own backyard.

Get Ready for Your Picnic

- **1 hour before leaving:** Put the cans of fruit juice into the refrigerator so they can be chilling. Or, make lemonade and chill it also.

- **30 minutes before leaving:** Prepare **BANANA DOGS** and Pickle Pops. Follow recipe directions at right for **BANANA DOGS.** To make Pickle Pops, use a table knife to cut off 1 end of 4 whole sweet or dill pickles. Insert a small wooden stick into cut end of each pickle. Wrap each in clear plastic wrap.

- **10 minutes before leaving:** Tie **BANANA DOGS,** Pickle Pops, apples, and cookies in bandannas. Tie the bandannas to sticks or old broom handles.

- **5 minutes before leaving:** Put the fruit juice into the picnic basket. If taking lemonade, pour it into an insulated container and put into basket. Pack plates, cups, and napkins. Don't forget a can opener for your fruit juice, if you need it!

BANANA DOGS

EQUIPMENT	INGREDIENTS
measuring cups and spoons	¾ cup creamy *or* chunk-style peanut butter
small mixing bowl	2 tablespoons honey
rubber scraper	4 hot dog buns, split
table knife	2 small bananas
cutting board	1 tablespoon lemon juice
custard cup	
pastry brush	
clear plastic wrap	

 Measure peanut butter and honey. Put them into a small mixing bowl. Stir peanut butter and honey together with a rubber scraper.

 Measure *3 tablespoons* of the peanut butter-honey mixture. Put the 3 tablespoons onto *one* hot dog bun. Use a table knife to spread the mixture evenly on the bun. Prepare the 3 other hot dog buns the same way.

 Peel the 2 small bananas. On a cutting board, use the table knife to cut both bananas in half, cutting from top to bottom.

 Measure the lemon juice. Put lemon juice into a custard cup. Use a pastry brush to brush the 4 banana halves with the lemon juice. (This will help keep the bananas from turning brown.) Place *one* banana half into *each* hot dog bun.

 Wrap each sandwich in clear plastic wrap. Makes 4 sandwiches.

CHOCOLATE-CHERRY DESSERT

EQUIPMENT

range top
measuring cups
  and spoons
plastic bag
rolling pin
8x8x2-inch
  baking dish
small bowl
small saucepan
fork
small spoon
small mixer bowl
electric mixer
rubber scraper
can opener
large spoon
clear plastic
  wrap

INGREDIENTS

26 chocolate
    wafers
¼ cup butter *or*
    margarine
 1 8-ounce carton
    dairy sour
    cream
 1 package
    4-serving-size
    instant choco-
    late pudding
    mix
1¼ cups milk
 1 21-ounce can
    cherry pie
    filling

WASH HANDS

1

Count out the chocolate wafers. Put 5 or 6 wafers at a time into a plastic bag. Close bag. Use a rolling pin to crush the wafers. Put the crushed chocolate wafers into an 8x8x2-inch baking dish. When all the wafers are crushed, measure 2 tablespoons of crumbs. Set the 2 tablespoons of crumbs aside in a small bowl till you're ready to use them.

2

ADULT HELP

Measure the butter or margarine and put it into a small saucepan. Put the pan onto the burner. Turn the burner to low heat. When the butter or margarine is melted, turn off the burner. Pour the melted butter or margarine over the crushed wafers in the baking dish.

3

Use a fork to stir together the crushed wafers and the melted butter or margarine. With your hands, spread the wafer mixture evenly over the bottom of the dish. Press the crumbs with your fingers to form a crust. Make sure the crust is the same thickness everywhere in the dish. Put the crust into the refrigerator for 30 minutes or into the freezer for 10 minutes or till it's firm.

Spoon the sour cream into a small mixer bowl. Add the dry pudding mix to mixer bowl. Measure milk and pour it into mixer bowl. Turn an electric mixer to low speed and beat about 1 minute or till mixture is smooth. Turn mixer off. Lift beaters out of bowl. Use a rubber scraper to scrape sides of bowl. Put beaters back into bowl. Turn mixer to low speed and beat 30 seconds more. Turn mixer off. Lift beaters out of bowl. Scrape beaters and sides of bowl. Use a measuring cup to scoop the mixture into baking dish. Use the rubber scraper to scrape out the bowl and to spread the pudding mixture over wafer crust.

Use a can opener to open the can of cherry pie filling. Carefully spoon the pie filling over the pudding layer. Sprinkle the 2 tablespoons chocolate wafer crumbs over the pie filling. Cover the dish with clear plastic wrap and put it into the refrigerator for 3 hours or into the freezer for 1 hour or till cold. Cut into squares to serve. Makes 9 servings.

4

ADULT HELP

5

USE YOUR MICROWAVE

Make short work of melting the butter or margarine in this recipe by doing it in your counter-top microwave oven! Unwrap the butter or margarine and put it into a 1-cup glass or plastic measuring cup or a custard cup. Micro-cook, uncovered, on high power about 40 seconds.

TRY IT THIS WAY

Vanilla-Peach Dessert: Follow the recipe for Chocolate-Cherry Dessert, *but* instead of the chocolate wafers, use 33 *vanilla wafers* for the crust. And instead of the chocolate pudding mix, use 1 package 4-serving-size *instant French vanilla pudding mix.* Spoon one 21-ounce can *peach pie filling* over pudding layer in place of the cherry pie filling.

CLEAN UP

EASY CHOCOLATE CAKE

EQUIPMENT

oven
measuring cups
  and spoons
13x9x2-inch
  baking pan
paper towel
large mixer bowl
small bowl
fork
rubber scraper
electric mixer
wooden pick
hot pads
cooling rack
narrow metal
  spatula

INGREDIENTS

½ cup butter *or*
  margarine
Shortening
1 tablespoon
  all-purpose
  flour
2 cups all-purpose
  flour
2 cups sugar
⅓ cup unsweet-
  ened cocoa
  powder
¾ teaspoon baking
  soda
¾ teaspoon baking
  powder
½ teaspoon ground
  cinnamon
2 eggs
¾ cup milk
¼ teaspoon almond
  extract
  (if you like)
¾ cup milk
  Canned choco-
  late frosting
  (if you like)

WASH HANDS

1 Soften the butter or margarine by setting it out of the refrigerator at least 30 minutes before making the chocolate cake so the butter or margarine will be easy to mix.

2 Grease the 13x9x2-inch baking pan by putting a little bit of shortening on a folded paper towel. Spread the shortening evenly over the bottom of the pan. Measure 1 tablespoon flour and put it into the greased pan. Tilt the pan back and forth and tap the side of it with your hand to spread the flour evenly over the bottom. Dump out any extra flour.

3 Turn oven to 350°. Measure the 2 cups flour, sugar, cocoa powder, baking soda, baking powder, and cinnamon. Put these dry ingredients into a large mixer bowl. Stir together with a rubber scraper.

4 Crack one of the eggs on the side of a small bowl. Working over the bowl, gently separate the eggshell halves and pour the egg into the bowl. Repeat with the second egg. Use a fork to beat eggs lightly till the yolks and whites are mixed well. Measure ¾ cup milk. Put softened butter or margarine, eggs, and milk into the mixer bowl. Measure the almond extract and add it to the mixer bowl, if you like.

This chocolate cake goes together in a flash, and it uses ingredients you're bound to have on hand!

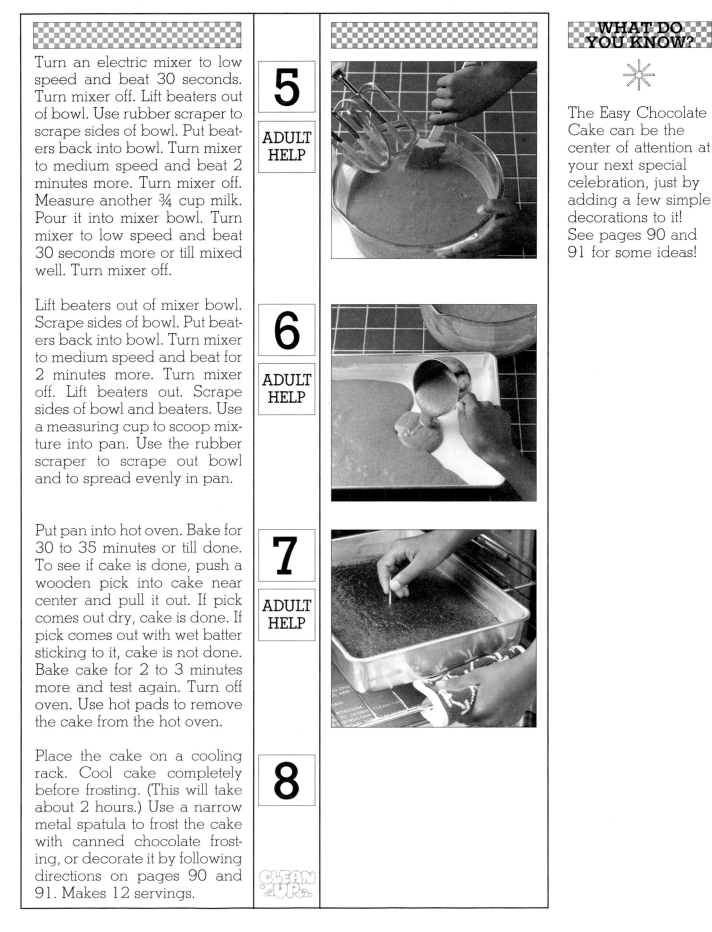

5 ADULT HELP

Turn an electric mixer to low speed and beat 30 seconds. Turn mixer off. Lift beaters out of bowl. Use rubber scraper to scrape sides of bowl. Put beaters back into bowl. Turn mixer to medium speed and beat 2 minutes more. Turn mixer off. Measure another ¾ cup milk. Pour it into mixer bowl. Turn mixer to low speed and beat 30 seconds more or till mixed well. Turn mixer off.

6 ADULT HELP

Lift beaters out of mixer bowl. Scrape sides of bowl. Put beaters back into bowl. Turn mixer to medium speed and beat for 2 minutes more. Turn mixer off. Lift beaters out. Scrape sides of bowl and beaters. Use a measuring cup to scoop mixture into pan. Use the rubber scraper to scrape out bowl and to spread evenly in pan.

7 ADULT HELP

Put pan into hot oven. Bake for 30 to 35 minutes or till done. To see if cake is done, push a wooden pick into cake near center and pull it out. If pick comes out dry, cake is done. If pick comes out with wet batter sticking to it, cake is not done. Bake cake for 2 to 3 minutes more and test again. Turn off oven. Use hot pads to remove the cake from the hot oven.

8

Place the cake on a cooling rack. Cool cake completely before frosting. (This will take about 2 hours.) Use a narrow metal spatula to frost the cake with canned chocolate frosting, or decorate it by following directions on pages 90 and 91. Makes 12 servings.

WHAT DO YOU KNOW?

The Easy Chocolate Cake can be the center of attention at your next special celebration, just by adding a few simple decorations to it! See pages 90 and 91 for some ideas!

CARAMEL CEREAL POPS

EQUIPMENT

range top
measuring cups
kitchen scissors
3-quart saucepan
wooden spoon
8x8x2-inch
  baking pan
paper towel
table knife
narrow metal
  spatula
16 wooden sticks

INGREDIENTS

1 14-ounce pack-
  age (about 48)
  vanilla
  caramels
¼ cup milk
4 cups crisp rice
  cereal
1 cup salted
  peanuts
Shortening

WASH HANDS

1

ADULT HELP

Use the kitchen scissors to cut open the package of caramels. Unwrap the caramels and put them into a heavy 3-quart saucepan. Measure the milk and add it to the pan with the caramels. Put the pan onto the burner. Turn burner to low heat. Cook and stir with a wooden spoon till caramels are melted and smooth. This will take about 15 minutes.

2

Turn burner off. Take pan off burner. Measure the crisp rice cereal and peanuts. Stir the cereal and peanuts into the pan. Keep stirring till the cereal and peanuts are well coated with the melted caramel mixture.

3

Grease an 8x8x2-inch baking pan by putting a little bit of shortening on a folded paper towel. Spread the shortening evenly over the bottom and sides of the pan. Spoon the cereal mixture into the pan. Use the back of the wooden spoon to press the cereal mixture into the pan. Let the mixture stand about 1 hour or till firm.

4

Use a table knife to cut the firm cereal mixture into 2-inch squares. Use the table knife or a narrow metal spatula to remove the 2-inch squares from the pan. Insert a wooden stick into one end of each square. Makes 16 pops.

CLEAN UP

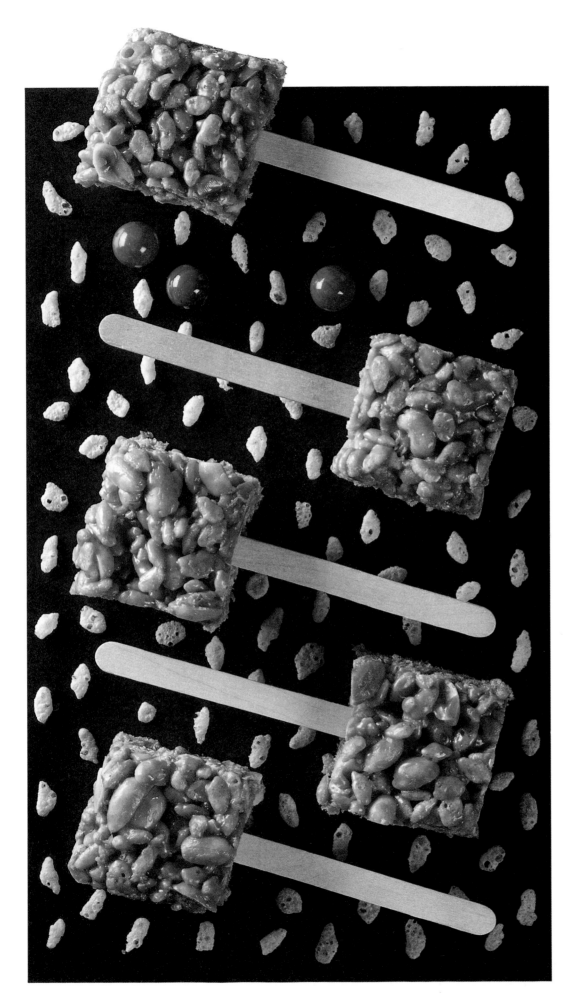

Melting the caramels for Caramel Cereal Pops goes much faster if you have a counter-top microwave oven! Unwrap the caramels and put them into a medium microwave-safe mixing bowl. Add the ¼ cup milk. Micro-cook, uncovered, on high power for 1½ minutes, then stir the mixture. Micro-cook on high power for 1 minute more. Stir again.

WHAT DO YOU KNOW?

If you don't have a microwave oven to melt the caramels, you may find that 15 minutes is a long time to stand at the range top stirring. You can play Tom Sawyer and get a brother or sister to take turns stirring with you. Or, ask Mom or Dad to take a turn!

JUNIOR SHORTCAKES

EQUIPMENT

oven
measuring cups
  and spoons
two 6-cup muffin
  pans *or* one
  12-cup muffin
  pan
paper towel
large mixing
  bowl
wooden spoon
pastry blender
rubber scraper
small mixing
  bowl
fork
large spoon
small spoon
hot pads
narrow metal
  spatula *or*
  table knife
cooling rack
small bowl
small spoon

INGREDIENTS

½ cup butter *or*
  margarine
  Shortening
2 cups all-purpose
  flour
2 tablespoons
  sugar
1 tablespoon
  baking powder
½ teaspoon salt
1 egg
⅔ cup milk
1 10-ounce jar
  strawberry jam
  or grape jelly
1 tablespoon
  lemon juice
  Pressurized
  dessert topping
  (if you like)

WASH HANDS

1 Soften the butter or margarine by setting it out of the refrigerator at least 30 minutes before making the shortcakes so the butter or margarine will be easy to mix.

2 Turn oven to 450°. Grease the muffin pan by putting a little bit of shortening on a folded paper towel. Spread shortening evenly over the bottom and sides of the muffin cups.

3 Measure the flour, the sugar, baking powder, and salt. Put them into a large mixing bowl. Stir with a wooden spoon till mixed well. Add the softened butter or margarine. With a pastry blender, use an up-and-down motion to mix the butter into the flour mixture. Stop once in a while and use a rubber scraper to remove any butter that sticks to the pastry blender. Mix till the pieces of butter or margarine are the size of small peas.

4 Crack the egg on the side of a small mixing bowl. Working over the bowl, gently separate the eggshell halves over the bowl and pour the egg into the bowl. Use a fork to beat the egg lightly till the yolk and white are mixed well. Measure the milk. Pour it into the bowl with the egg. Stir gently till milk and egg are mixed well.

5 Pour the egg-milk mixture into the flour mixture. Stir with the wooden spoon till the dry ingredients are wet. The batter should be lumpy, so do not stir too much.

Your friends will be tickled when you serve them these tender, individual shortcakes as a snack!

43

6

To spoon the batter into the greased muffin cups, get enough of the batter on a large spoon so it is slightly humped in the spoon. With the back of a small spoon, push batter into the muffin cups. Fill each cup about ½ full with batter.

7

ADULT HELP

Put muffin pan into the hot oven. Bake for 12 to 15 minutes or till the shortcakes are golden. Turn off oven. Use hot pads to remove the muffin pan from the oven. Cool the shortcakes in the pan for 10 minutes. Using a narrow metal spatula or table knife, carefully remove the shortcakes from the muffin cups. Let the shortcakes cool on a cooling rack.

8

While the shortcakes are cooling, make the filling mixture for the shortcakes. Spoon the strawberry jam or grape jelly into a small bowl. Measure lemon juice and add to the bowl with jam or jelly. Stir with the spoon till mixed well.

9

Use the narrow metal spatula or the table knife to cut the cooled shortcakes in half through the middle. Spoon a little bit of the filling mixture on the bottom halves of the shortcakes. Put the tops back on the shortcakes and spoon on more filling mixture. Top each shortcake with a little bit of the dessert topping, if you like. Makes 12 shortcakes.

TRY IT THIS WAY

Applesauce Shortcakes: Follow the recipe for Junior Shortcakes, *but* try a different filling mixture. In a small bowl stir together 1½ cups *chunk-style applesauce* and ½ teaspoon ground *cinnamon*. Spoon this mixture in the centers and over the tops of the cooled shortcakes instead of the jam or jelly mixture.

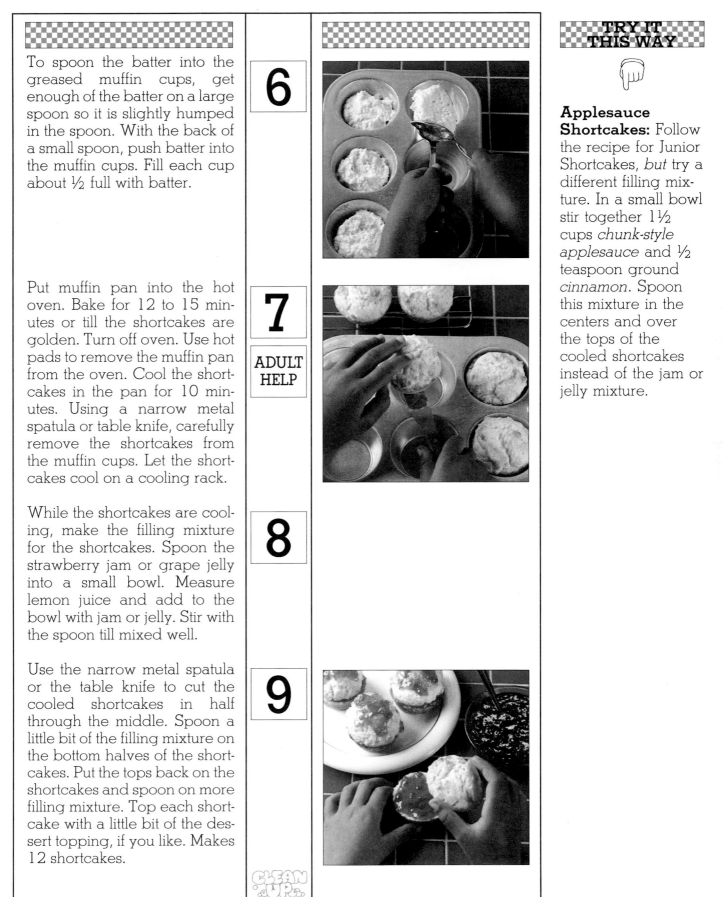

POTATO SALAD

EQUIPMENT

range top
measuring cups
3-quart saucepan
  with lid
vegetable brush
fork
slotted spoon
1-quart saucepan
  with lid
bowl
cutting board
sharp knife
ruler
large mixing
  bowl
egg slicer
table knife
rubber scraper
kitchen scissors

INGREDIENTS

5 cups water
5 medium
  potatoes
2 eggs
  Cold water
  Ice water
2 stalks celery
2 green onions
½ cup creamy
  cucumber salad
  dressing
  Parsley

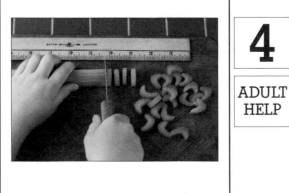

WASH HANDS

1 ADULT HELP

Measure the water. Put it into a 3-quart saucepan. Rinse the potatoes in cold water. Scrub the potatoes thoroughly with a vegetable brush. Put potatoes into pan with water. Put pan onto burner. Turn burner to high heat. When the water starts to boil, turn burner to low heat and put the lid onto pan.

2 ADULT HELP

Cook the potatoes for 30 to 40 minutes or till tender. (Poke the potatoes with a fork to see if they are tender.) Turn off burner. Remove pan from burner. Carefully take the lid off the saucepan. (Be careful because steam can come rolling out and burn you.) Using a slotted spoon, remove potatoes from pan. Set potatoes aside.

3 ADULT HELP

To hard-cook eggs, carefully put them into the 1-quart pan. Add enough cold water to pan to cover eggs. Put pan onto burner. Turn burner to high heat. When water just begins to boil, turn burner to low heat. Put lid on pan. Cook eggs for 15 minutes. Turn burner off. Remove the pan from burner. Carefully take lid off pan. Using slotted spoon, take eggs out of pan. Put eggs into a bowl filled with ice water.

4 ADULT HELP

Rinse celery stalks and green onions in cold water. On a cutting board, use a sharp knife to trim off leaves and ends of celery stalks. Cut stalks into slices about ¼ inch thick. Use a ruler to check size of slices. Hold celery on cutting board with round side up so it doesn't roll around as you're cutting it.

5

On the cutting board, use the sharp knife to trim off the roots and ends of the green onions. Pull off any withered leaves. Cut the green onions into slices about ¼ inch thick. Hold the onion tightly as you cut it because it will try to roll away from you! Put the sliced celery and sliced green onion into a large mixing bowl.

6

To remove the shells from the cooled hard-cooked eggs, roll the eggs over the counter top. This cracks the shells into lots of little pieces. Start at the largest end of the egg and peel off the pieces of shell. The shells should come off easily. If they don't want to come off, try holding the egg under cold running water while peeling away the shell.

7

A fun and fast way to cut the eggs into nice, even slices is to use an egg slicer! Put one of the peeled, hard-cooked eggs into the slicer. Pull the slicing wires down through the egg. Add the sliced egg to the large mixing bowl. Repeat with the second egg. (If you don't have an egg slicer, on the cutting board, use a sharp knife to cut the hard-cooked eggs into thin slices.)

(CONTINUED on next page)

If you're planning to take Potato Salad with you on a picnic, you want to be sure it stays very cold. The best way to do this is to pack it in an insulated cooler, surrounded by lots of ice.

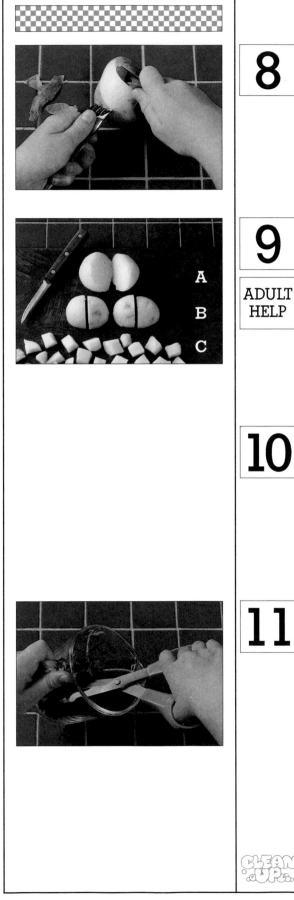

8 Gently poke the fork into one of the warm potatoes to hold it as you peel off the skin. Use a table knife to scrape and peel away the potato skin. Repeat with the remaining potatoes. Throw away the peelings.

9 **ADULT HELP** (**A**) On the cutting board, use the sharp knife to cut one of the peeled potatoes in half. (**B**) Put the flat sides of the cut potato halves down. Cut each potato half in half again. Now the potato is in 4 pieces. (**C**) Cut each piece into ½-inch cubes. Repeat with the remaining potatoes. Add the potato cubes to the large bowl.

10 Measure the cucumber dressing. Pour the dressing over the ingredients in the bowl. Use a rubber scraper to carefully stir the dressing into the ingredients till mixed well. Cover the bowl. Put the potato salad into the refrigerator for 3 to 4 hours or till it's cold.

11 Use kitchen scissors to cut the stems off a small bunch of parsley. Put the parsley into a measuring cup. Snip the parsley into small pieces. Before serving the potato salad, sprinkle the snipped parsley over the top of the potato salad. The parsley is an attractive way to "dress up" your potato salad. Makes 4 to 6 servings.

CLEAN UP

MARSHMALLOW CLOUDS

1

Soften frozen whipped dessert topping by setting it out of the freezer while you're getting the other ingredients together.

2

Put a strainer on top of a small bowl. Use a can opener to open the can of fruit cocktail. Empty the fruit cocktail into the strainer to drain (save the juice to use another time). Put the drained fruit cocktail into a large mixing bowl.

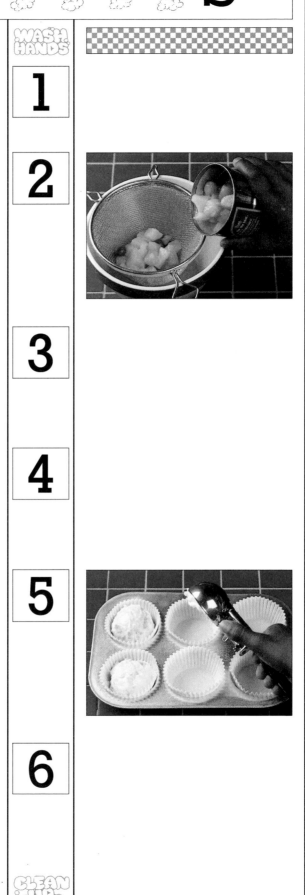

3

Measure the tiny marshmallows, strawberry yogurt, and mayonnaise or salad dressing. Add to the mixing bowl with the drained fruit. Use a rubber scraper to mix well.

4

Use the rubber scraper to empty the container of thawed whipped dessert topping into the bowl with the fruit mixture. Stir the dessert topping into the fruit mixture till mixed well.

5

Line the muffin pans with paper bake cups (you'll only use 8 of the muffin cups). Use an ice cream scoop or a large spoon to put the fruit mixture into the paper bake cups. Put the muffin pans into the freezer. Freeze till salads are firm. This will take about 2 hours.

6

Before serving the frozen salads, rinse lettuce leaves. Pat dry with a paper towel. Put a lettuce leaf onto each salad plate. Remove the paper bake cups from the salads and put a salad onto each salad plate. Let the salads stand for 15 to 20 minutes so they will soften slightly. Makes 8 servings.

EQUIPMENT

measuring cups
 and spoons
strainer
small bowl
can opener
large mixing
 bowl
rubber scraper
two 6-cup
 muffin pans *or*
 one 12-cup
 muffin pan
8 paper bake
 cups
ice cream scoop
 or large spoon
paper towel

INGREDIENTS

1 4-ounce con-
 tainer frozen
 whipped des-
 sert topping
1 16-ounce can
 fruit cocktail
½ cup tiny
 marshmallows
½ cup strawberry
 yogurt
2 tablespoons
 mayonnaise *or*
 salad dressing
Lettuce leaves

WHAT DO YOU KNOW?

If you have any extra *Marshmallow Clouds*, put them into a plastic bag and store them in the freezer.

ADULT HELP

Purple Cows

Soften 1 pint (2 cups) *vanilla ice cream* by setting it out of the freezer while you're getting the other ingredients together. Use a can opener to open one 6-ounce can *frozen grape juice concentrate*. Use a rubber scraper to empty the can of concentrate into a blender container. Measure 1¼ cups *milk*. Add milk to blender container. Spoon the softened ice cream into blender container. Cover the blender. Blend till smooth. Turn off the blender. Serve at once. Makes 4 (8-ounce) servings.

Slushy Fruit Fizzes

Soften one 6-ounce can *frozen pineapple juice concentrate* by setting it out of the freezer while you're getting the other ingredients together. Measure 1½ cups *orange juice*, 1½ cups *water*, and 1 tablespoon *honey*. Pour into a 2-quart pitcher. Use a can opener to open the can of concentrate. Add to pitcher. Stir till mixed well. Use a fork to mash 1 medium *banana*. Stir mashed banana into pitcher; mix well. Pour mixture into a 9x5x3-inch loaf pan. Cover with foil. Put into freezer till frozen. (It will take about 6 hours to freeze.)

To serve, remove the frozen mixture from freezer. Let stand about 20 minutes or till you're able to scrape the top with a spoon to form a slush. For each serving, measure ⅔ cup slush. Put slush into a tall glass. Fill glasses with *lemon-lime soda pop*. Freeze remaining slush. Makes 9 (8-ounce) servings.

Banana Smoothies

On a cutting board, use a table knife to cut 2 medium *bananas* into 1-inch pieces. Wrap the banana pieces in clear plastic wrap or foil. Freeze the banana pieces till firm. (This will take several hours.)

Measure 1½ cups *milk*. Pour milk into a blender container. Add an 8-ounce carton *plain yogurt* to blender container. Measure 2 tablespoons *sugar* and 1 teaspoon *vanilla*. Add to blender container.

Put *half* of the frozen banana pieces into the blender container. Cover the blender and blend till mixed well. Turn off the blender. Add the remaining frozen banana pieces and cover the blender. Blend till smooth. Turn off the blender. Serve at once. Makes 4 (8-ounce) servings.

Hot Chocolate Mix

Measure 5½ cups *nonfat dry milk powder*, 2½ cups *presweetened cocoa powder*, 2 cups *tiny marshmallows*, and ¾ cup *powdered non-dairy creamer*. Put ingredients into a bowl. Put in 3 tablespoons *ground cinnamon* if you would like a spicy mix.) Use a spoon to stir till mixed well. Put ingredients into an airtight container to store. Makes about 9½ cups mix (enough for 28 servings).

To use *Hot Chocolate Mix*, measure ⅓ *cup* mix for each serving. Put mix into a mug or cup. Measure ¾ cup hot *water*. Add hot water to mug or cup. Stir till mix dissolves.

ADULT HELP

VEGGIES WITH DILLY DIP

EQUIPMENT

measuring cups
  and spoons
paper towels
bowl
vegetable peeler
cutting board
sharp knife
ruler
fork
blender
rubber scraper

INGREDIENTS

Assorted vegeta-
  bles such as
  carrots, celery,
  cauliflower,
  cucumbers, *or*
  green peppers
Ice cubes
Cold water
1 cup cream-style
  cottage cheese
¼ cup mayonnaise
  or salad
  dressing
2 tablespoons milk
1 teaspoon dried
  dillweed
1 teaspoon minced
  dried onion

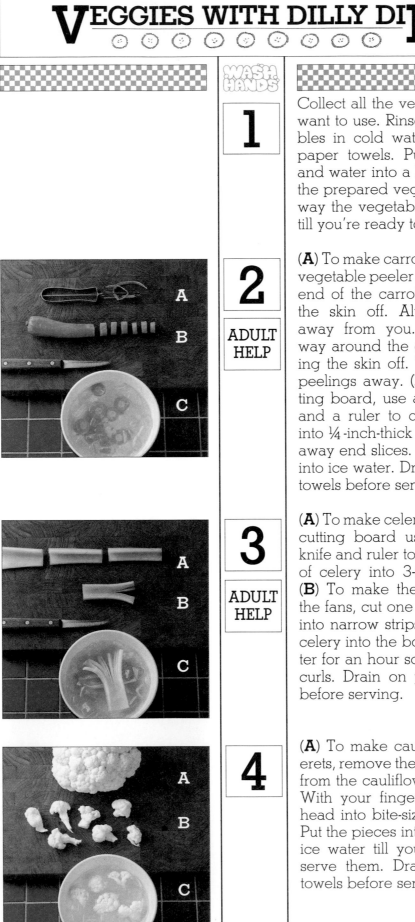

WASH HANDS

1

Collect all the vegetables you want to use. Rinse the vegetables in cold water. Drain on paper towels. Put ice cubes and water into a bowl to store the prepared vegetables. This way the vegetables stay crisp till you're ready to use them.

2

ADULT HELP

(**A**) To make carrot coins, use a vegetable peeler to start at one end of the carrot and scrape the skin off. Always scrape away from you. Work your way around the carrot, scraping the skin off. Throw carrot peelings away. (**B**) On a cutting board, use a sharp knife and a ruler to cut the carrot into ¼-inch-thick slices. Throw away end slices. (**C**) Put slices into ice water. Drain on paper towels before serving.

3

ADULT HELP

(**A**) To make celery fans, on the cutting board use the sharp knife and ruler to cut the stalks of celery into 3-inch lengths. (**B**) To make the "fringe" on the fans, cut one or both ends into narrow strips. (**C**) Put the celery into the bowl of ice water for an hour so the "fringe" curls. Drain on paper towels before serving.

4

(**A**) To make cauliflower flowerets, remove the green leaves from the cauliflower head. (**B**) With your fingers, break the head into bite-size pieces. (**C**) Put the pieces into the bowl of ice water till you're ready to serve them. Drain on paper towels before serving.

The more you dunk these crunchy vegetables into the dip, the better they get!

51

(**A**) To make fancy cucumber slices, on a cutting board use a sharp knife to cut a small slice off both ends of cucumber. Throw away end slices. (**B**) Run a fork down cucumber from end to end. Press hard enough to break skin. Make this design with fork all the way around cucumber. Cut cucumber into thin slices. (**C**) Put into ice water. Drain on paper towels before serving.

(**A**) To make green pepper strips, on a cutting board use sharp knife to cut green pepper in half from top to bottom. Use your fingers to pull off and throw away the stem. Remove and throw away seeds and soft white parts from inside both halves. (**B**) Place the rounded sides of green pepper halves down on the cutting board. Cut one half into ½-inch-thick strips. Repeat with the other green pepper half. (**C**) Put strips into ice water. Drain on paper towels before serving.

To make the dilly dip, measure the *undrained* cottage cheese, mayonnaise or salad dressing, milk, dillweed, and dried onion. Put ingredients into a blender container. Cover the blender and blend till smooth. Turn off blender. Uncover and use a rubber scraper to scrape down the sides of the blender container.

Arrange drained vegetables on a platter. Pour dip into a small serving bowl; serve with vegetables. Makes 1 cup dip.

5 ADULT HELP

6 ADULT HELP

7 ADULT HELP

8

CLEAN UP

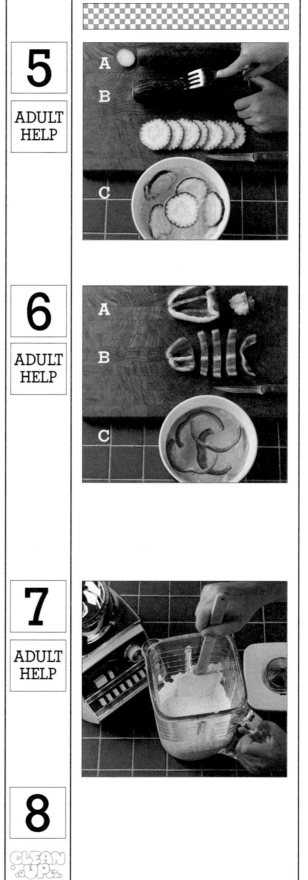

WHAT DO YOU KNOW?

Snacks can taste good and be good for you, too. Try to choose foods that help supply required nutrients.

Cheese, for example, provides protein. Carrots, cherry tomatoes, and the other vegetables used in *Veggies with Dilly Dip* all contribute vitamins. The milk products used to make the *Dilly Dip* help supply calcium.

CHEESY MACARONI SOUP

EQUIPMENT

range top
measuring cups
  and spoons
3-quart saucepan
  with lid
colander
wooden spoon
kitchen scissors
can opener

INGREDIENTS

6 cups water
½ teaspoon salt
1 7¼-ounce pack-
  age macaroni
  and cheese
  dinner mix
1 10-ounce
  package
  frozen mixed
  vegetables
¼ cup butter *or*
  margarine
¼ cup all-purpose
  flour
2 13¾-ounce cans
  chicken broth
1½ cups milk

WASH HANDS

1 ADULT HELP

Measure water and salt. Put into a 3-quart saucepan. Put pan onto burner. Turn burner to high heat. When the water starts to boil, carefully add the macaroni from the packaged dinner mix. Cover the pan with the lid. Cook for 5 minutes. Remove the lid and carefully add the frozen mixed vegetables. When the water starts to boil again, turn burner to low heat. Cover the pan with the lid. Cook for 5 minutes more.

2 ADULT HELP

To drain the cooked macaroni and vegetables, put a colander into the sink. Carefully pour the macaroni and vegetables out of the saucepan into the colander. (Be very careful because steam will rise out of the sink as you pour out the macaroni and vegetables, and it can be very hot.) Let macaroni and vegetables stand a few minutes to drain well.

3 ADULT HELP

Measure the butter or margarine. Put butter or margarine into the same 3-quart saucepan that you used before. Put pan onto burner. Turn burner to medium heat. Measure the flour. When butter or margarine is melted, use a wooden spoon to stir in the flour. Stir till smooth. Use kitchen scissors to cut open the package of cheese sauce mix from the packaged dinner mix. Pour the cheese sauce mix into the saucepan. Use the wooden spoon to stir till mixed well.

Use a can opener to open the cans of chicken broth. Pour broth into pan. Use the wooden spoon to stir till smooth. Measure milk. Slowly stir the milk into the pan. Cook and stir till mixture boils. (This will take 6 to 8 minutes.) Once it starts to boil, cook and stir for 1 minute more.

Turn burner to medium-low heat. Carefully stir the drained macaroni and vegetables into the pan. Cook for 1 to 2 minutes or till the soup is heated through. Turn burner off. Take pan off burner. Ladle soup into bowls. Serve soup with a sandwich. Makes 6 servings.

4

ADULT HELP

5

ADULT HELP

CLEAN UP

POPCORN MUNCHIES

EQUIPMENT

range top
oven
measuring cups
13x9x2-inch
  baking pan
small saucepan
rubber scraper
hot pads
wooden spoon
kitchen scissors
glass
pancake turner

INGREDIENTS

6 cups popped
  popcorn
1 cup dry roasted
  peanuts
⅓ cup shredded
  coconut
2 tablespoons
  butter *or*
  margarine
¼ cup honey
¾ cup dried
  apricots
¾ cup raisins

WASH HANDS

1 Pour the popped popcorn into a 13x9x2-inch baking pan. Measure the peanuts and the coconut. Add the peanuts and the coconut to the baking pan. Do not stir yet, or the popcorn will crumble too much.

2 **ADULT HELP** Measure the butter or margarine. Put butter or margarine into a small saucepan. Put pan onto burner. Turn burner to low heat. When the butter or margarine melts, turn off burner. Take pan off burner. Measure the honey. Use a rubber scraper to stir the honey into melted butter or margarine.

3 Drizzle the butter-honey mixture over the popcorn mixture in the baking pan. Gently stir the mixture with the rubber scraper till mixed well.

4 **ADULT HELP** Put the baking pan into the oven. Turn oven to 300°. Bake for 20 minutes. Once or twice, while the mixture is baking, use hot pads to remove the pan from the oven and stir the popcorn mixture with a wooden spoon. Use hot pads to put the pan back into hot oven.

5 While the popcorn mixture is in the oven, use kitchen scissors to snip the dried apricots into small pieces. (If your scissors start sticking together, dip the scissor blades into a glass of cold *water.*) Set the snipped apricots aside till you're ready to use them. Measure the raisins and set aside also.

Turn off oven. Use hot pads to remove pan from oven. Cool slightly. Loosen mixture with a pancake turner. Stir apricots and raisins into popcorn mixture. Pour the popcorn mixture into a large serving bowl. Makes 7 cups.

6

ADULT HELP

CLEAN UP

✳

Have you ever made popcorn in a saucepan on the range top instead of using an electric popcorn popper? Ask an adult to help you, and here's what you do:

Pour 3 tablespoons *cooking oil* into a heavy 3-quart saucepan. Add 2 or 3 kernels *unpopped popcorn.*

Put the pan onto the burner. Turn burner to medium-high heat. Put the lid on the pan and cook till you hear the corn pop.

Remove the lid and add ⅓ cup *unpopped popcorn.* Put the lid back on and cook, shaking the pan gently.

When the popping slows down, turn off the burner. Shake till the corn stops popping.

Empty the popcorn into a bowl. Measure the amount you need for *Popcorn Munchies* (6 cups), being careful not to use any unpopped kernels.

TUNA-CHEESE PATTIES

EQUIPMENT

broiler
measuring cups
  and spoons
strainer
bowl
can opener
rubber scraper
fork
mixing bowl
plastic bag
rolling pin
waxed paper
ruler
table knife
broiler pan and
  rack
paper towel
pancake turner
hot pads
toaster

INGREDIENTS

1 6½-ounce can
  tuna *or* one 6¾-
  ounce can
  chunk-style
  chicken
1 egg
¼ cup milk
2 teaspoons dried
  parsley flakes
14 saltine crackers
2 ¾-ounce slices
  American *or*
  Swiss cheese
Shortening
4 slices whole
  wheat, white,
  or rye bread,
  or 2 English
  muffins, split
4 lettuce leaves
4 tomato slices
  (if you like)

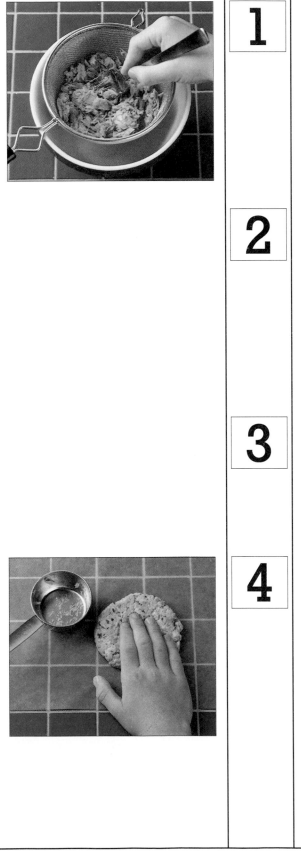

WASH HANDS

1 Place a strainer onto a bowl. Use a can opener to open the can of tuna or chicken. Use a rubber scraper to empty the tuna or chicken into the strainer. Use a fork to break the tuna or chicken into chunks.

2 Crack the egg on the side of a mixing bowl. Working over the bowl, gently separate the eggshell halves and pour the egg into the bowl. Measure the milk and parsley flakes. Put them into the bowl with the egg. Beat with the fork till mixed well. Put the tuna or chicken into bowl. Use rubber scraper to stir till mixed well.

3 Count out the crackers. Put the crackers into the plastic bag. Close the bag. Use a rolling pin to crush the crackers. Add the crushed crackers to mixing bowl with the tuna or chicken mixture. Stir till mixed well.

4 Measure *⅓ cup* of the tuna or chicken mixture. Working on waxed paper, use your hands to shape the mixture into a flat, round patty, about 3½ inches wide. Repeat with the remaining tuna or chicken mixture. (You'll have 4 patties.) On a cutting board, use a table knife to cut one of the cheese slices in half from corner to corner to make 2 triangles. Repeat with the second slice of cheese. Set the 4 cheese triangles aside till you're ready to use them.

5 Grease the rack of a broiler pan by putting a little bit of shortening on a folded paper towel. Spread shortening generously over rack. Use a pancake turner to carefully lift tuna or chicken patties off waxed paper and onto greased rack.

6 Before turning the broiler on, put the broiler pan under the broiler. Use a ruler to make sure the patties are about 3 inches from the broiler coils or burner. If you need to, move the oven rack up or down so the patties are just the right distance from the broiler coils or burner.

7 **ADULT HELP** Turn broiler on. Cook for 3 to 4 minutes or till patties are golden brown. Use hot pads to remove the broiler pan from the broiler. Use the pancake turner to loosen the patties from broiler rack. Turn patties over with pancake turner. Use hot pads to put broiler pan back under the broiler. Cook about 3 minutes or till brown. Turn off broiler. Use hot pads to remove the broiler pan from the broiler. Quickly place *one* cheese triangle on *each* patty.

8 Meanwhile, use a toaster to toast bread or English muffins. Place *one* lettuce leaf on top of a slice of toast or an English muffin half. Put a patty on top of lettuce. Top with *one* tomato slice, if you like. Prepare the 3 other sandwiches the same way. Makes 4 sandwiches.

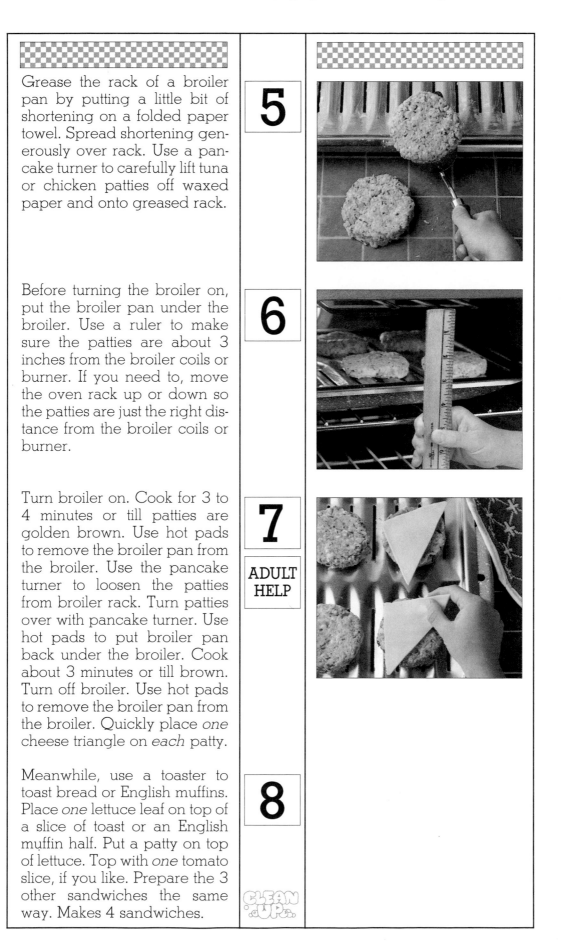

DAISY BISCUITS

EQUIPMENT

oven
measuring cups
 and spoons
mixing bowl
wooden spoon
pastry blender
rubber scraper
pastry cloth *or*
 waxed paper
rolling pin
ruler
custard cup
2½-inch biscuit
 cutter
kitchen scissors
pancake turner
cookie sheet
hot pads

INGREDIENTS

¼ cup butter *or*
 margarine
1 3-ounce package
 cream cheese
2 cups all-purpose
 flour
1 tablespoon
 baking powder
½ teaspoon salt
¾ cup milk
 All-purpose flour
 Your favorite jam
 or jelly

WASH HANDS

1 Soften the butter and cream cheese by setting them out of the refrigerator at least 30 minutes before making the biscuits. This will make the butter and cream cheese easy to mix.

2 Measure the 2 cups flour, baking powder, and salt. Put them into a mixing bowl. Stir with a wooden spoon till mixed well. Add softened butter or margarine and cream cheese. With a pastry blender, use an up-and-down motion to mix the butter and cream cheese with the flour mixture. Stop once in a while and use a rubber scraper to remove any butter or cream cheese that sticks to the pastry blender. Mix till pieces of butter and cream cheese are the size of small peas.

3 Measure the milk. Add the milk to the flour mixture. Stir with the wooden spoon just till the dry ingredients are wet. Do not stir the dough too much or the biscuits will be tough. Sprinkle a pastry cloth or sheet of waxed paper with *3 or 4 teaspoons* flour.

4 Spoon the dough out of the mixing bowl and onto the pastry cloth or waxed paper. Turn the dough over to coat it with flour. Use your hands to shape it into a ball. Sprinkle a little flour onto a rolling pin. Use the rolling pin to roll out the dough on the pastry cloth or waxed paper to make a 12x7-inch rectangle. (Dough will be slightly less than ½ inch thick.) Use a ruler to check the size.

5

Turn oven to 450°. Put *2 or 3 tablespoons* flour into a custard cup. Dip a 2½-inch biscuit cutter into flour and then cut the dough into biscuits by pressing down firmly on the biscuit cutter. Cut the biscuits as close together as possible. Dip the biscuit cutter into flour after you cut each biscuit. This will stop the dough from sticking to the biscuit cutter.

6

Carefully lift scraps of dough from around cut biscuits. Set this extra dough aside to roll out again for more biscuits.

7

To make the daisy design, use the kitchen scissors to make 5 small cuts around the edge of each biscuit. *Do not* cut all the way to the center. Use a pancake turner to lift the daisy biscuits onto a cookie sheet. Roll out the scraps of dough. Cut more biscuits and make daisy design in these biscuits too.

8

Press your thumb into the center of each biscuit to make a hole. Spoon ½ *teaspoon* of your favorite jam or jelly into the center of *each* biscuit.

9

ADULT HELP

Put the cookie sheet into the hot oven. Bake for 10 to 12 minutes or till golden. Turn off oven. Use hot pads to remove the cookie sheet from oven. With pancake turner, lift biscuits off cookie sheet and onto a serving plate. Serve warm. Makes 13 or 14 biscuits.

CHEESY VEGETABLE BAKE

EQUIPMENT

range top
oven
measuring cups
  and spoons
2-quart saucepan
  with lid
wooden spoon
colander
can opener
rubber scraper
large bowl
kitchen scissors
10x6x2-inch
  baking dish
hot pads

INGREDIENTS

½ cup water
2 10-ounce pack-
  ages of your
  favorite frozen
  vegetable
1 10¾-ounce can
  condensed
  cream of celery
  soup
¼ cup milk
1 4-ounce pack-
  age (1 cup)
  shredded ched-
  dar cheese
½ teaspoon dried
  basil
1 8-ounce pack-
  age (12 rolls)
  refrigerated
  flaky dinner
  rolls

WASH HANDS

1

ADULT HELP

Measure the water. Pour water into the 2-quart saucepan. Put the pan onto the burner. Turn burner to high heat. When the water starts to boil, add the frozen vegetables.

2

ADULT HELP

When the water starts to boil again, turn burner to low heat. Cover the pan with the lid. Cook the vegetables, using the timing from the package. Once or twice during cooking, uncover the saucepan and stir the vegetables with a wooden spoon to break up any frozen clumps. Turn off the burner.

3

ADULT HELP

To drain the vegetables, put a colander into the sink. Carefully pour the vegetables out of the saucepan into the colander. (Be very careful because steam will rise out of the sink as you pour out the vegetables and can be very hot.)

4

Use a can opener to open the can of soup. Use a rubber scraper to empty the soup into a large bowl. Measure milk and add it to the bowl with soup. Use kitchen scissors to cut open the package of cheese. Add the cheese to the soup mixture. Add vegetables to soup mixture. Measure the dried basil. Crush it between your fingers as you sprinkle it over soup mixture. (Crushing any dried herb releases the flavor.) Use the rubber scraper to stir ingredients till mixed well.

This easy casserole can taste different every time you make it if you just vary the vegetables you put in it.

61

5

Spoon or pour the vegetable mixture into a 10x6x2-inch baking dish. Use the rubber scraper to scrape any remaining mixture out of the bowl and into the baking dish.

6

Put the baking dish into the oven. Turn oven to 350°. Bake about 20 minutes or till the vegetable mixture is bubbling around the edges.

7

ADULT HELP

Meanwhile, to open the flaky dinner rolls, follow the package directions. Use your fingers to separate the dinner roll dough into 12 pieces. Use the kitchen scissors to cut each of the 12 pieces in half. Now you have 24 pieces. Use hot pads to remove the hot baking dish from the oven. Quickly place the 24 dough pieces around the edges of the baking dish, with cut edges touching edges of dish. Use hot pads to put the dish back into the hot oven.

8

ADULT HELP

Bake about 20 minutes longer or till the roll pieces are golden brown. Turn off oven. Use hot pads to remove the baking dish from the oven. Makes 8 side dish servings.

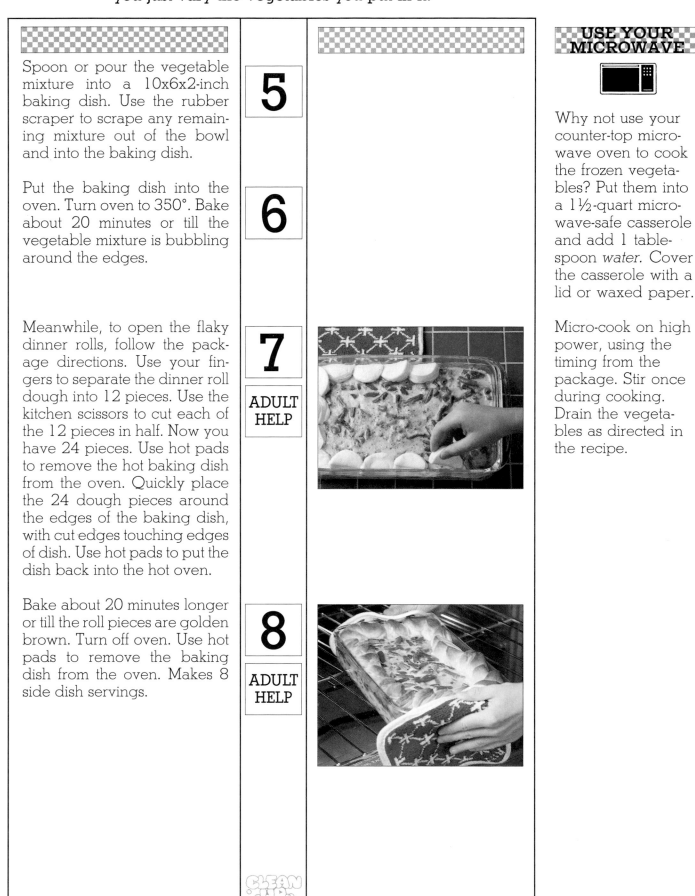

USE YOUR MICROWAVE

Why not use your counter-top microwave oven to cook the frozen vegetables? Put them into a 1½-quart microwave-safe casserole and add 1 tablespoon *water.* Cover the casserole with a lid or waxed paper.

Micro-cook on high power, using the timing from the package. Stir once during cooking. Drain the vegetables as directed in the recipe.

CLEAN UP

Not-the-Same-Old Grilled Cheese Sandwiches

Use a table knife to spread a little *butter or margar[ine]* on 4 slices of *whole wheat bread* (1 side only). Place *2* slices of bread, buttered sides down, in a 10-inch skillet. Put on 1 slice *Swiss cheese* onto each slice of bread in skillet. Sprinkle some *sunflower nuts* over cheese. Place another slice of whole wheat bread, buttered side up, on the sunflower nuts.

Put skillet onto burner. Turn burner to medium-low heat. Cook sandwiches till the bottom bread slices are toasted and golden. This will take about 8 minutes. Use a pancake turner to turn sandwiches over. Cook till the bottom bread slices are toasted and golden. This will take about 2 minutes. Turn off burner. Use the pancake turner to remove the sandwiches from the skillet. Makes 2 sandwiches.

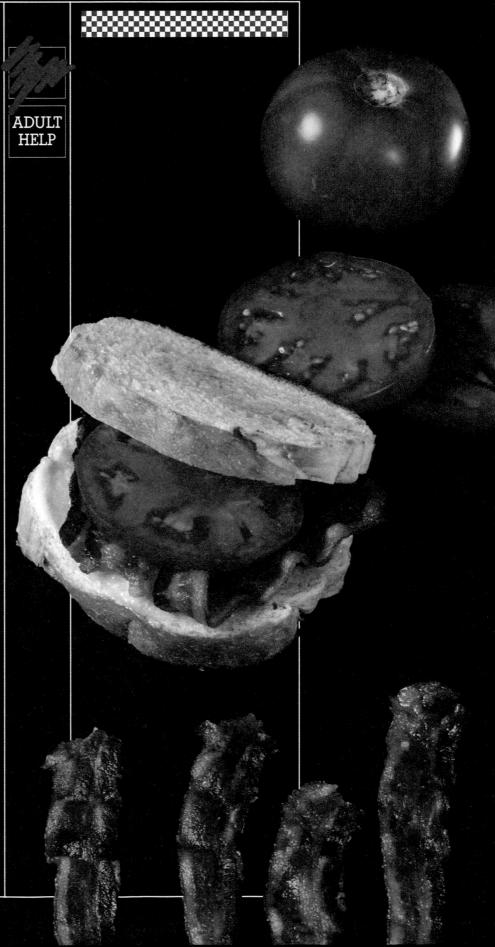

Bacon and Tomato
Sandwich Specials

Put slices of *bacon* side by side into a medium skillet. Put the skillet onto burner. Turn burner to medium-low heat. Cook bacon for 6 to 8 minutes or till crisp, turning often with tongs. Turn off burner. Use tongs to remove bacon from skillet. Put the cooked bacon onto paper towels to drain.

On a cutting board, use a sharp knife to cut 2 slices off a medium *tomato*.

Measure 2 tablespoons *mayonnaise or salad dressing* and 1 tablespoon grated *Parmesan cheese*. Put the mayonnaise or salad dressing and the Parmesan cheese into a small mixing bowl. Use a spoon to stir till mixed well.

Use a toaster to toast 4 thin slices of *French bread*. Use a table knife to spread a little *butter or margarine* on *each* slice of toast (1 side only).

For one sandwich, use a table knife to spread *half* of the mayonnaise mixture over the buttered side of *one* slice of toast. Put *two* slices of bacon on top of the mayonnaise mixture. Put *one* thin tomato slice on top of the bacon. Put another slice of toast, buttered side down, on top of the tomato. Make another sandwich the same way. Serve the sandwiches at once. Makes 2 sandwiches.

ADULT
HELP

64

GUMDROP NUT BREAD

EQUIPMENT

oven
measuring cups
 and spoons
9x5x3-inch loaf
 pan
paper towel
kitchen scissors
glass
large mixing
 bowl
plastic bag
rolling pin
wooden spoon
small mixing
 bowl
fork *or* rotary
 beater
rubber scraper
wooden pick
hot pads
cooling rack
narrow metal
 spatula *or*
 table knife

INGREDIENTS

Shortening
¾ cup tiny
  gumdrops
½ cup walnut
  pieces
 3 cups all-purpose
  flour
¾ cup sugar
 1 tablespoon
  baking powder
¼ teaspoon salt
 1 egg
1⅓ cups milk
⅓ cup cooking oil
½ teaspoon vanilla

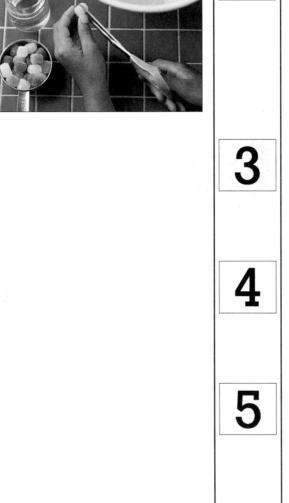

WASH HANDS

1 Turn oven to 350°. Grease the loaf pan by putting a little bit of shortening on a folded paper towel. Spread the shortening evenly over the bottom and sides of the loaf pan, being sure to get in the corners. Set the pan aside till you're ready to use it.

2 Measure the tiny gumdrops. Using kitchen scissors, snip the gumdrops in half. (If your scissors start sticking together, dip the blades into a glass of cold *water.*) Put snipped gumdrops into a large mixing bowl.

3 Measure the walnuts. Put the nuts into a plastic bag. Close the bag. Use a rolling pin to crush the nuts. Put the crushed walnuts into the mixing bowl with the gumdrops.

4 Measure the flour, sugar, baking powder, and salt. Put into the mixing bowl with the gumdrops and nuts. Stir with a wooden spoon till mixed well. Set aside till ready to use.

5 Crack the egg on the side of a small mixing bowl. Working over the bowl, gently separate the eggshell halves and pour the egg into the bowl. Use a fork to beat the egg lightly till the yolk and white of the egg are mixed well. Measure the milk, oil, and vanilla. Add to the bowl with the egg. Stir with the fork or rotary beater till mixed well.

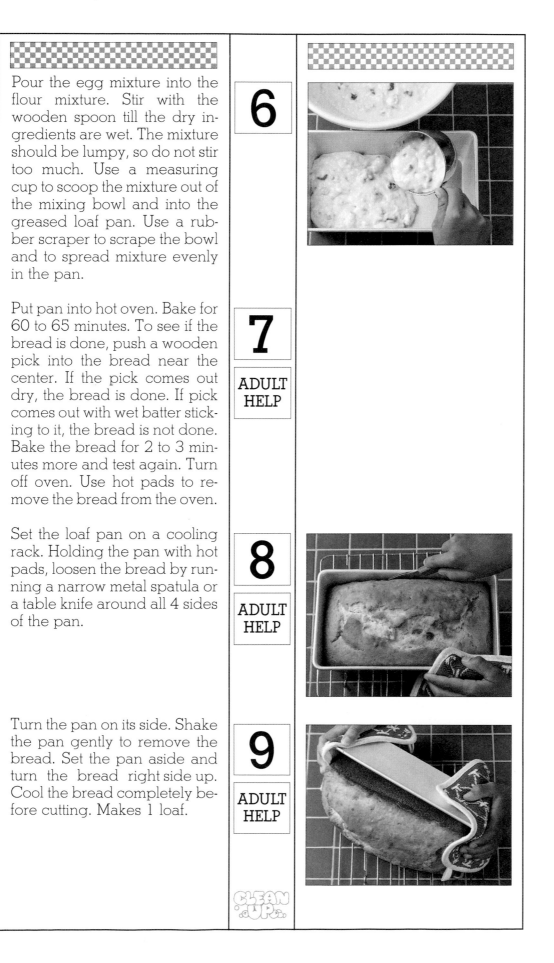

6 Pour the egg mixture into the flour mixture. Stir with the wooden spoon till the dry ingredients are wet. The mixture should be lumpy, so do not stir too much. Use a measuring cup to scoop the mixture out of the mixing bowl and into the greased loaf pan. Use a rubber scraper to scrape the bowl and to spread mixture evenly in the pan.

7 **ADULT HELP** Put pan into hot oven. Bake for 60 to 65 minutes. To see if the bread is done, push a wooden pick into the bread near the center. If the pick comes out dry, the bread is done. If pick comes out with wet batter sticking to it, the bread is not done. Bake the bread for 2 to 3 minutes more and test again. Turn off oven. Use hot pads to remove the bread from the oven.

8 **ADULT HELP** Set the loaf pan on a cooling rack. Holding the pan with hot pads, loosen the bread by running a narrow metal spatula or a table knife around all 4 sides of the pan.

9 **ADULT HELP** Turn the pan on its side. Shake the pan gently to remove the bread. Set the pan aside and turn the bread right side up. Cool the bread completely before cutting. Makes 1 loaf.

CLEAN UP

TASTY TACOS

EQUIPMENT

range top
measuring cups
  and spoons
cutting board
sharp knife
10-inch skillet
wooden spoon
long-handled
  spoon
can *or* container
  for grease
can opener
rubber scraper
paper towels
kitchen scissors
spoon

INGREDIENTS

1 small onion
1 pound ground
  beef
1 10¾-ounce can
  condensed
  tomato soup
¼ cup water
1 teaspoon chili
  powder
1 teaspoon pre-
  pared mustard
1 teaspoon
  Worcestershire
  sauce
¼ teaspoon garlic
  salt
3 *or* 4 lettuce
  leaves
1 4-ounce package
  (1 cup) shred-
  ded cheddar
  cheese
8 to 10 taco shells
  Pitted black
  olives, sliced
  (if you like)
  Dairy sour cream
  (if you like)
Taco sauce

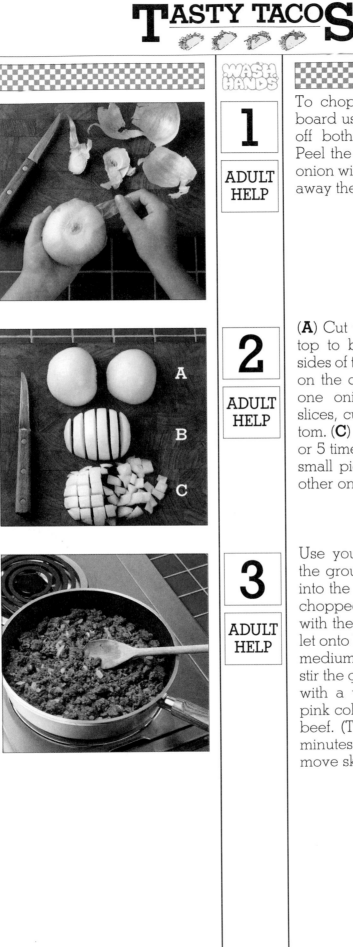

WASH HANDS

1 ADULT HELP

To chop onion, on a cutting board use a sharp knife to cut off both ends of the onion. Peel the outside skin from the onion with your fingers. Throw away the skin and end pieces.

2 ADULT HELP

(**A**) Cut the onion in half from top to bottom. Place the cut sides of the onion halves down on the cutting board. (**B**) Cut one onion half into several slices, cutting from top to bottom. (**C**) Cut across the slices 4 or 5 times to cut the onion into small pieces. Repeat with the other onion half.

3 ADULT HELP

Use your hands to break up the ground beef as you put it into the 10-inch skillet. Put the chopped onion into the skillet with the ground beef. Put skillet onto burner. Turn burner to medium-high heat. Cook and stir the ground beef and onion with a wooden spoon till no pink color is left in the ground beef. (This will take about 10 minutes.) Turn off burner. Remove skillet from burner.

Tasty Tacos are pictured on the front cover.

4 ADULT HELP

Use a long-handled spoon to push the ground beef to one side of the skillet. Tip the skillet a little bit so the grease runs to the other side. Use the long-handled spoon to carefully put the grease into a can or container an adult gives you. (Be careful because both the skillet and the grease will be hot.)

5

Use a can opener to open can of soup. Use a rubber scraper to empty soup into skillet with ground beef. Measure the water, the chili powder, mustard, Worcestershire sauce, and garlic salt. Add to skillet; mix.

6 ADULT HELP

Put skillet onto burner. Turn burner to high heat. Cook till mixture boils, stirring several times with wooden spoon. When it starts to boil, turn burner to low heat. Cook till mixture thickens, stirring a few times. (This will take 5 to 7 minutes.) Turn off burner.

7

While meat mixture is cooking, rinse lettuce in cold water. Pat lettuce dry with paper towels. Use your fingers to tear lettuce into bite-size pieces. Use kitchen scissors to cut open the package of shredded cheese.

8

To serve, use a spoon to put some of the meat mixture into each taco shell. Add lettuce and cheese. If you like, put olive slices and sour cream on top of cheese. Top with taco sauce. Repeat with remaining tacos. Makes 8 to 10 tacos.

CLEAN UP

MENU
FAMILY SUPPER

Porcupine Meatballs

Lettuce Salads

Green Beans

Dinner rolls

Ice cream
with caramel topping

Iced tea or milk

Every now and then, moms and dads need a break in their daily routines. An offer from you to do the cooking some night no doubt would be a pleasant surprise!

Before you begin, read through both of these pages to make sure you understand everything. Check the ingredient and equipment lists to be sure you have everything you need. (This menu feeds four or five people.)

You can buy the dinner rolls from a bakery, or your local supermarket may have a bakery section that has dinner rolls.

When setting the table, you'll need a plate, glass, fork, knife, spoon, and napkin for each person. Keep the salad plates and the bowls for the ice cream in the kitchen because you'll be working with them. Put some butter or margarine on the table to serve with the dinner rolls.

Making the table look pretty is very important. Try making a centerpiece from something simple—a bowl of fresh fruit, a bouquet of spring flowers, or even a pretty candle.

When everyone has finished, clear the table and serve the ice cream with caramel topping.

Get Ready for Supper

- **1 hour and 15 minutes before serving:** Prepare **PORCUPINE MEATBALLS.** Follow the recipe directions at right.

- **40 minutes before serving:** Start cooking **PORCUPINE MEATBALLS.** Set the table.

- **30 minutes before serving:** To prepare Lettuce Salads, rinse the lettuce under cold water. Place on paper towels to drain. Tear the lettuce into bite-size pieces and fill 4 or 5 salad plates. For some added crunch, slice your favorite fresh vegetable (this could be carrots or celery or whatever you like) and add to the lettuce. Top with cherry tomato halves and croutons. To make the salads extra special, add some fresh bean sprouts, too. Drizzle the salads with your favorite bottled dressing. Place the salad plates on the table.

- **15 minutes before serving:** To heat Green Beans, use a can opener to open a 16-ounce can French-style green beans. Put beans into a small saucepan. Put the pan onto burner. Turn the burner to medium-low heat. Cover the pan with a lid and cook for 15 minutes.

- **10 minutes before serving:** Scoop ice cream into 4 or 5 bowls. Put bowls into freezer to keep frozen while you're eating supper.

- **At serving time:** Pour iced tea or milk. If you like, serve each glass of tea with a halved lemon slice. Put rolls into a basket; set on the table. Put the **PORCUPINE MEATBALLS** and Green Beans into serving containers. Place on table. Before serving ice cream for dessert, drizzle caramel topping on top.

PORCUPINE MEATBALLS

EQUIPMENT	INGREDIENTS
range top	1 egg
measuring cups and spoons	1 10¾-ounce can condensed tomato soup
large mixing bowl	¼ cup long grain rice
fork	1 tablespoon dried parsley flakes
can opener	1 teaspoon minced dried onion
rubber scraper	¼ teaspoon salt
wooden spoon	Dash pepper
10-inch skillet with lid	1 pound lean ground beef
small mixing bowl	½ cup water
	1 teaspoon Worcestershire sauce

1 Crack the egg on the side of a large mixing bowl. Working over the bowl, gently separate the eggshell halves and pour the egg into the bowl. Use a fork to beat the egg lightly till mixed well. Use a can opener to open the can of tomato soup. Measure ¼ *cup* of tomato soup. Use a rubber scraper to stir the ¼ cup of soup into the beaten egg.

2 Measure the *uncooked* rice, parsley flakes, dried onion, salt, and pepper. Add to egg-soup mixture in the large mixing bowl. Use a wooden spoon to stir till mixed well. Add ground beef; mix well. Use your hands to shape meat mixture into 1-inch meatballs. You should have about 20 meatballs. Put the meatballs into a 10-inch skillet.

3 Measure the water. Put water into a small mixing bowl. Use the rubber scraper to empty the rest of soup into the mixing bowl. Measure Worcestershire sauce. Add to mixing bowl. Use the rubber scraper to stir till mixed well. Pour the soup mixture over the meatballs in the skillet.

4 ADULT HELP Put skillet onto burner. Turn burner to medium-high heat. When mixture starts to boil, turn burner to low heat. Cover the skillet with the lid. Cook for 40 minutes. Use the wooden spoon to carefully stir the meatballs often, so they don't stick to the skillet. Turn off burner. Makes 4 or 5 servings.

MENU
WEEKEND BRUNCH

Polka-Dot Oven Pancake

Bubbling Fruit

Milk

Some lazy Sunday morning, why not fix brunch for your family? Brunch is a meal that is a combination of breakfast and lunch. It is usually eaten later in the morning than breakfast.

Tell your family you're fixing pancakes and sausages. Won't they be surprised when they discover that you're making one giant square pancake and that it bakes in the oven? And what's even more fun is that the sausage cooks in the pancake!

Before you begin, read through both of these pages to make sure you understand everything.

Check the ingredient and equipment lists to be sure you have everything you need. (This menu will feed four to six people.)

When setting the table, you'll need a plate, glass, fork, knife, spoon, and napkin for each person. You'll also need a small bowl for each person (for the fruit). Keep these bowls in the kitchen where you're preparing the food. Don't forget to put butter and maple syrup on the table for the pancake squares!

After you've eaten brunch, be sure to clean up the kitchen.

Get Ready for Brunch

- **1 hour before serving:** To prepare Bubbling Fruit, use a can opener to open one 8¾-ounce can peach slices and one 8-ounce can pineapple chunks (juice pack). Drain the can of peach slices. Throw away the juice. Put peach slices into a bowl. Add the pineapple chunks to the bowl (add the pineapple juice, too).

  Measure ½ cup seedless green grapes. On a cutting board, use a sharp knife to cut grapes in half. Add them to the bowl. Peel and slice 1 medium banana. Add banana slices to bowl. Measure ¼ cup flaked coconut and add to bowl. Use a wooden spoon to stir the fruit till mixed well. Cover the bowl and put it into the refrigerator to chill till serving time.

- **50 minutes before serving:** Prepare **POLKA-DOT OVEN PANCAKE.** Follow recipe directions at right.

- **30 minutes before serving:** Put the **POLKA-DOT OVEN PANCAKE** into the oven. Set the table.

- **5 minutes before serving:** Remove the **POLKA-DOT OVEN PANCAKE** from the oven. Cut the pancake into 4 to 6 squares and place on a serving platter. Set the pancake squares, butter, and syrup on the table.

- **At serving time:** Pour the milk. Spoon the chilled fruit mixture into individual serving bowls. For a bubbly effect, measure ½ cup chilled ginger ale. Pour a little ginger ale over each serving and watch it bubble!

POLKA-DOT OVEN PANCAKE

EQUIPMENT

range top
oven
measuring cups and spoons
cutting board
sharp knife
small skillet
wooden spoon
paper towels
large mixing bowl
small mixing bowl
fork
small saucepan
11x7x1½-inch baking pan
hot pads

INGREDIENTS

1 8-ounce package brown-and-serve sausage links
1 cup all-purpose flour
2 tablespoons sugar
2 teaspoons baking powder
¼ teaspoon salt
1 egg
¾ cup milk
3 tablespoons butter *or* margarine
Shortening

 On a cutting board, use a sharp knife to cut sausage into ½-inch-thick slices. Put sausage into a small skillet. Put skillet onto burner. Turn to medium heat. Cook till brown, stirring once in a while with a wooden spoon. Turn off burner. Use spoon to remove sausage from skillet. Drain on paper towels.

1 ADULT HELP

 Turn oven to 375°. Measure the flour, sugar, baking powder, and salt. Put them into a large mixing bowl. Crack the egg on side of a small mixing bowl. Working over bowl, gently separate the eggshell halves and pour egg into bowl. Use a fork to beat egg lightly. Measure milk. Stir into egg.

2

 Measure butter. Put into small saucepan. Put pan onto burner. Turn burner to low heat. When butter melts, turn off burner. Pour melted butter into bowl with egg mixture; stir till mixed. Pour egg mixture into flour mixture. Stir with wooden spoon till dry ingredients are wet. The mixture should be lumpy.

3 ADULT HELP

 Grease an 11x7x1½-inch baking pan with a little shortening. Pour batter into greased pan; sprinkle with sausage. Put pan into hot oven. Bake about 25 minutes or till golden. Turn off oven. Use hot pads to remove pan from oven. To serve, cut into squares. Makes 4 to 6 servings.

4 ADULT HELP

LEMON-BERRY FREEZER PIE

EQUIPMENT

range top
measuring cups
 and spoons
plastic bag
rolling pin
mixing bowl
small saucepan
rubber scraper
9-inch pie plate
spoon

INGREDIENTS

18 graham cracker
 squares
 6 tablespoons
 butter *or*
 margarine
 2 tablespoons
 sugar
 1 pint lemon
 sherbet
 1 4-ounce con-
 tainer frozen
 whipped dessert
 topping
 ⅓ cup seedless red
 raspberry jam

WASH HANDS

1 Count out the graham cracker squares. Put 6 graham cracker squares at a time into a plastic bag. Close the bag. Use a rolling pin to crush the crackers. Pour the crushed crackers into a mixing bowl.

2 **ADULT HELP** Measure the butter or margarine. Put the butter or margarine into a small saucepan. Put saucepan onto burner. Turn burner to low heat. When the butter or margarine melts, turn off the burner. Pour the melted butter or margarine into the mixing bowl with the crushed graham crackers.

3 Measure the sugar and add it to the mixing bowl with the crushed crackers and the melted butter or margarine. Use a rubber scraper to stir the mixture till it's mixed well.

4 Pour crumb mixture into a 9-inch pie plate. Use your hands to spread crumbs evenly in pie plate. Pat the mixture onto the bottom and sides of the pie plate. Try to make sure the crumb mixture is the same thickness on the bottom and sides. Put the piecrust into refrigerator for 45 minutes or into freezer for 15 minutes or till crust becomes firm.

5

Soften the sherbet and frozen whipped dessert topping by setting them out of the freezer at least 15 minutes before making the filling for the pie. This will make the sherbet and dessert topping easy to use.

6

Remove the chilled piecrust from the refrigerator or freezer. Measure the raspberry jam. Use a spoon to dot the bottom of the chilled crust with raspberry jam:

7

Use the spoon to stir the sherbet till it's evenly thawed and smooth. Spread the sherbet evenly over the jam. Use the spoon to dot the top of the pie with the thawed whipped dessert topping.

8

Put the pie into the freezer. Freeze for 4 to 6 hours or overnight. Remove the pie from the freezer 20 to 30 minutes before serving so it can soften. Makes 8 servings.

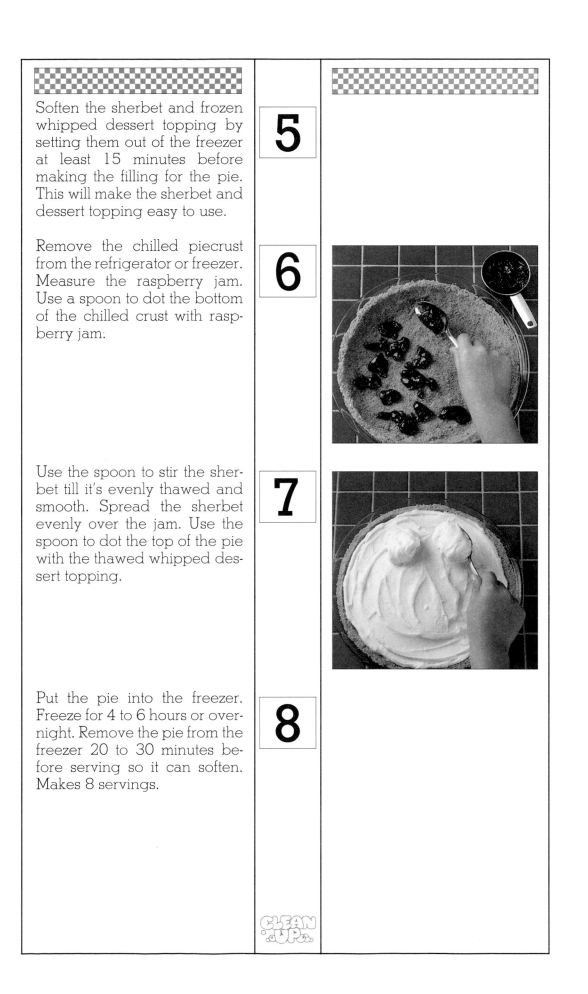

CLEAN UP

No-Cook-Noodles Lasagna

EQUIPMENT

range top
oven
measuring cups
  and spoons
10-inch skillet
wooden spoon
long-handled
  spoon
can *or* container
  for grease
rubber scraper
waxed paper
shredder
mixing bowl
fork
12x7½x2-inch
  baking dish
spoon
foil
hot pads
tongs

INGREDIENTS

1 pound ground
  beef
1 15½-ounce jar
  spaghetti sauce
6 ounces (1½ cups
  shredded) moz-
  zarella cheese
2 eggs
1½ cups cream-style
  cottage cheese
¼ cup grated
  Parmesan
  cheese
1 teaspoon dried
  oregano
9 lasagna noodles
¾ cup hot water

WASH HANDS

1 ADULT HELP

Use your hands to break up the ground beef as you put it into a 10-inch skillet. Put skillet onto burner. Turn the burner to medium-high heat. Cook and stir ground beef with a wooden spoon till no pink color is left. Turn off burner. Take skillet off burner. Use a long-handled spoon to push the ground beef to one side of pan. Tip skillet a little so grease runs to other side. Use spoon to carefully put grease into can or container an adult gives you. (Be careful because skillet and grease will be hot.)

2

Open jar of spaghetti sauce. Use a rubber scraper to empty spaghetti sauce into skillet with ground beef. Stir with wooden spoon till mixed well.

3 ADULT HELP

Put a sheet of waxed paper under the shredder to catch the cheese as you shred it. Hold the shredder with one hand and move the mozzarella cheese down across shredder to cut it into long, thin pieces.

4

Crack one of the eggs on the side of a mixing bowl. Working over the bowl, gently separate the eggshell halves and pour egg into the bowl. Repeat with the second egg. Use a fork to beat eggs lightly till the yolks and whites of the eggs are mixed well. Measure the cottage cheese, Parmesan cheese, and *1 cup* of the shredded cheese. Add to the eggs. Measure the oregano. Crush it between your fingers as you sprinkle it over bowl. Mix egg-cheese mixture well.

The noodles go in "stiff as a board," but come out cooked and tender in this no-fuss lasagna.

75

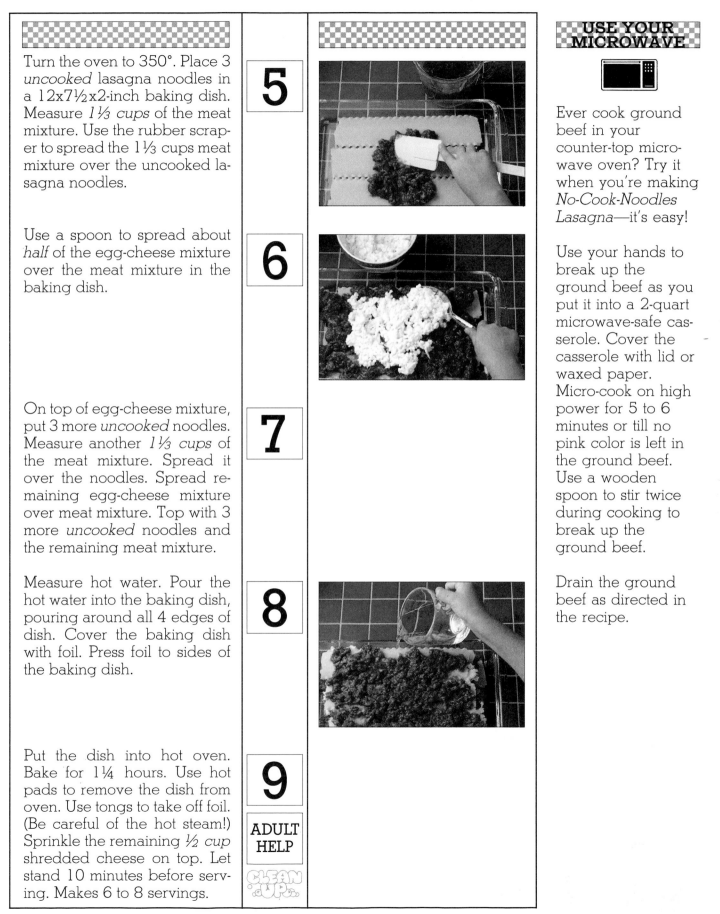

Turn the oven to 350°. Place 3 *uncooked* lasagna noodles in a 12x7½x2-inch baking dish. Measure *1⅓ cups* of the meat mixture. Use the rubber scraper to spread the 1⅓ cups meat mixture over the uncooked lasagna noodles.

5

Use a spoon to spread about *half* of the egg-cheese mixture over the meat mixture in the baking dish.

6

On top of egg-cheese mixture, put 3 more *uncooked* noodles. Measure another *1⅓ cups* of the meat mixture. Spread it over the noodles. Spread remaining egg-cheese mixture over meat mixture. Top with 3 more *uncooked* noodles and the remaining meat mixture.

7

Measure hot water. Pour the hot water into the baking dish, pouring around all 4 edges of dish. Cover the baking dish with foil. Press foil to sides of the baking dish.

8

Put the dish into hot oven. Bake for 1¼ hours. Use hot pads to remove the dish from oven. Use tongs to take off foil. (Be careful of the hot steam!) Sprinkle the remaining ½ cup shredded cheese on top. Let stand 10 minutes before serving. Makes 6 to 8 servings.

9

ADULT HELP

CLEAN UP

USE YOUR MICROWAVE

Ever cook ground beef in your counter-top microwave oven? Try it when you're making *No-Cook-Noodles Lasagna*—it's easy!

Use your hands to break up the ground beef as you put it into a 2-quart microwave-safe casserole. Cover the casserole with lid or waxed paper. Micro-cook on high power for 5 to 6 minutes or till no pink color is left in the ground beef. Use a wooden spoon to stir twice during cooking to break up the ground beef.

Drain the ground beef as directed in the recipe.

STICKY CINNAMON ROLLS

EQUIPMENT

range top
oven
measuring cups
  and spoons
thermometer
kitchen scissors
fork
mixing bowl
wooden spoon
small saucepan
rubber scraper
9x1½-inch round
  baking pan
plastic bag
rolling pin
small bowl
large spoon
small spoon
saucepan
hot pads
table knife

INGREDIENTS

⅔ cup warm water
1 package active
  dry yeast
2 cups packaged
  biscuit mix
¼ cup packed
  brown sugar
2 tablespoons
  butter *or*
  margarine
1 tablespoon light
  corn syrup
⅓ cup pecan halves
¼ cup sugar
½ teaspoon ground
  cinnamon

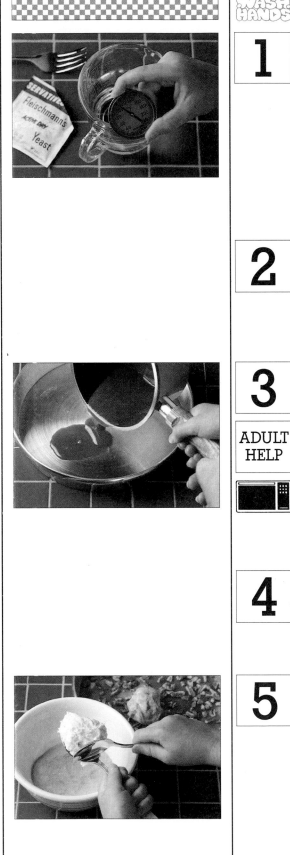

WASH HANDS

1 Measure warm water. Check water temperature with a thermometer. The water must be 115°. (This temperature is warm enough for yeast to grow and make rolls rise, but not so hot that it will kill yeast.) Use kitchen scissors to cut open package of yeast. Use a fork to stir yeast into warm water. Stir till yeast dissolves.

2 To make dough, measure biscuit mix. Put it into a mixing bowl. Pour yeast mixture into the bowl. Stir with a wooden spoon till mixed well. Set the dough aside.

3 **ADULT HELP** Measure brown sugar, butter, and corn syrup. Put into a small saucepan. Put pan onto burner. Turn burner to medium heat. Cook and stir sugar mixture with a rubber scraper till butter melts. Turn off burner. Pour sugar mixture into a 9x1½-inch round baking pan. Use rubber scraper to spread mixture over bottom of pan.

4 Measure the pecans. Put pecans into a plastic bag. Close bag. Use rolling pin to crush pecans. Sprinkle pecans over sugar mixture in pan.

5 Measure sugar and cinnamon. Put them into a small bowl. Stir till mixed well. Get enough dough on a large spoon so dough is slightly humped in spoon. With back of a small spoon, push dough into sugar-cinnamon mixture. Use small spoon to roll dough around in sugar-cinnamon mixture till it is well coated. Put coated balls of dough into baking pan.

Nothing goes better with these warm, gooey cinnamon rolls than a big glass of cold milk.

77

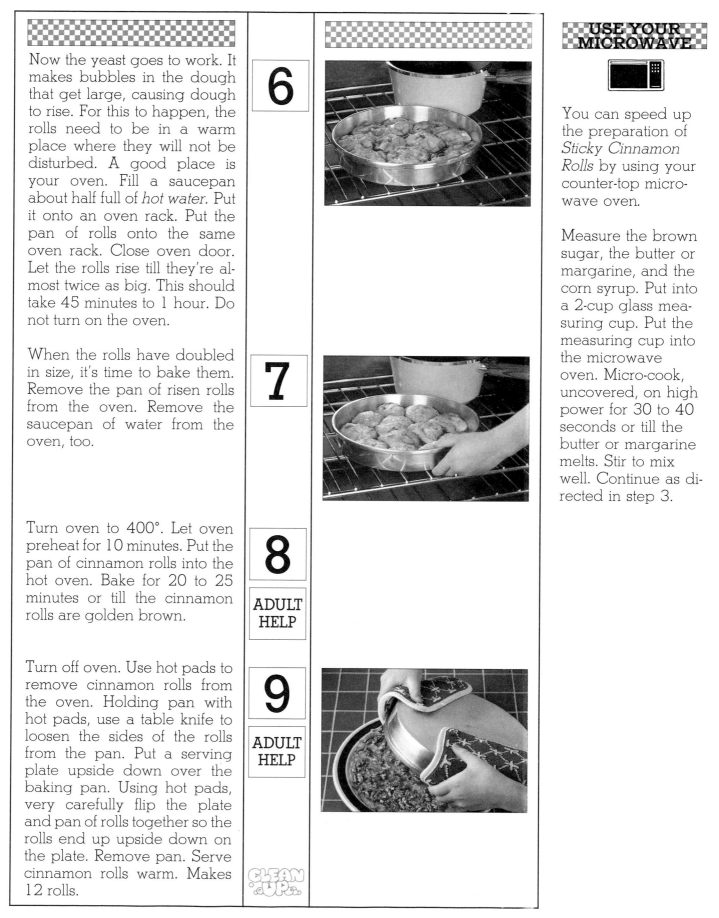

6

Now the yeast goes to work. It makes bubbles in the dough that get large, causing dough to rise. For this to happen, the rolls need to be in a warm place where they will not be disturbed. A good place is your oven. Fill a saucepan about half full of *hot water*. Put it onto an oven rack. Put the pan of rolls onto the same oven rack. Close oven door. Let the rolls rise till they're almost twice as big. This should take 45 minutes to 1 hour. Do not turn on the oven.

7

When the rolls have doubled in size, it's time to bake them. Remove the pan of risen rolls from the oven. Remove the saucepan of water from the oven, too.

8

ADULT HELP

Turn oven to 400°. Let oven preheat for 10 minutes. Put the pan of cinnamon rolls into the hot oven. Bake for 20 to 25 minutes or till the cinnamon rolls are golden brown.

9

ADULT HELP

Turn off oven. Use hot pads to remove cinnamon rolls from the oven. Holding pan with hot pads, use a table knife to loosen the sides of the rolls from the pan. Put a serving plate upside down over the baking pan. Using hot pads, very carefully flip the plate and pan of rolls together so the rolls end up upside down on the plate. Remove pan. Serve cinnamon rolls warm. Makes 12 rolls.

USE YOUR MICROWAVE

You can speed up the preparation of *Sticky Cinnamon Rolls* by using your counter-top microwave oven.

Measure the brown sugar, the butter or margarine, and the corn syrup. Put into a 2-cup glass measuring cup. Put the measuring cup into the microwave oven. Micro-cook, uncovered, on high power for 30 to 40 seconds or till the butter or margarine melts. Stir to mix well. Continue as directed in step 3.

WHOLE WHEAT TWIST LOAF

EQUIPMENT

range top
oven
measuring cups
  and spoons
large mixer bowl
kitchen scissors
wooden spoon
small saucepan
thermometer
freestanding
  electric mixer
rubber scraper
pastry cloth
cloth for
  covering dough
8x4x2-inch loaf
  pan
paper towel
ruler
saucepan
foil
hot pads
cooling rack
table knife

INGREDIENTS

1¾ to 2¼ cups all-
  purpose flour
1 package active
  dry yeast
1¼ cups milk
2 tablespoons
  sugar
2 tablespoons
  butter or
  margarine
½ teaspoon salt
1½ cups whole
  wheat flour
Shortening

WASH HANDS

1 Measure *1½ cups* of the all-purpose flour. Put flour into a large mixer bowl. Use kitchen scissors to cut open the package of yeast. Add yeast to mixer bowl. Use a wooden spoon to stir till mixed well.

2 ADULT HELP Measure milk, sugar, butter or margarine, and salt. Put into a small saucepan. Put pan onto burner. Turn burner to medium heat. Cook and stir with the wooden spoon till the butter melts and the mixture is warm (115°). Check the temperature of the mixture with a thermometer. (This 115° temperature is warm enough for the yeast to grow and make the bread rise, but not so hot that it will kill the yeast.) When the temperature reaches 115°, turn off the burner. Take pan off burner.

3 ADULT HELP Pour warm milk mixture over flour mixture in mixer bowl. Turn the electric mixer to low speed and beat for 30 seconds. Turn off mixer. Use a rubber scraper to scrape the sides of the mixer bowl.

4 ADULT HELP Turn mixer to high speed and beat for 3 minutes. Mixture should be smooth and mixed well. Turn off mixer. Use the rubber scraper to scrape the sides of the mixer bowl and the beaters.

5 Measure whole wheat flour. Use the wooden spoon to stir whole wheat flour into mixture in mixer bowl. As you add this flour, the dough will become stiff and get harder to stir.

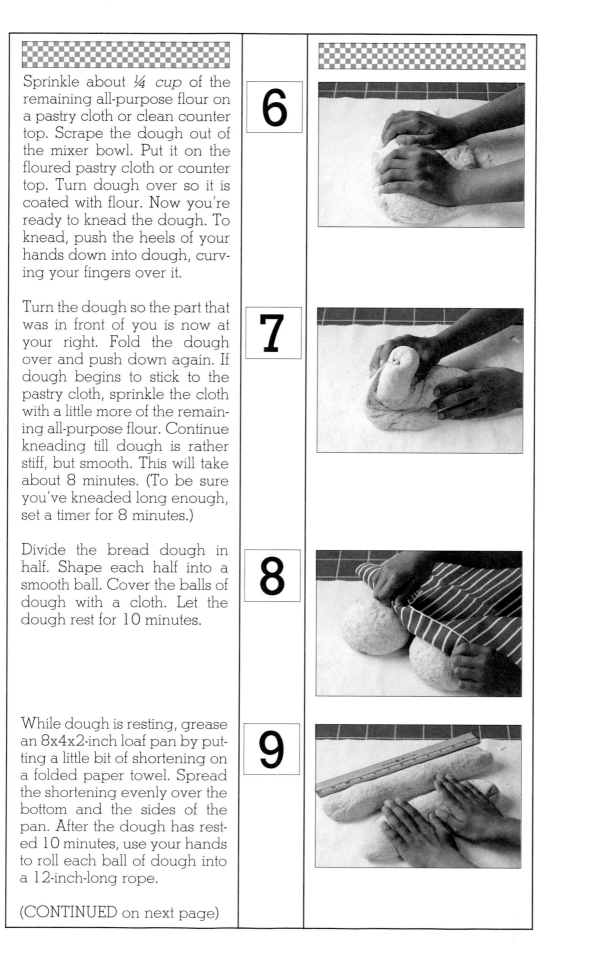

6 Sprinkle about ¼ *cup* of the remaining all-purpose flour on a pastry cloth or clean counter top. Scrape the dough out of the mixer bowl. Put it on the floured pastry cloth or counter top. Turn dough over so it is coated with flour. Now you're ready to knead the dough. To knead, push the heels of your hands down into dough, curving your fingers over it.

7 Turn the dough so the part that was in front of you is now at your right. Fold the dough over and push down again. If dough begins to stick to the pastry cloth, sprinkle the cloth with a little more of the remaining all-purpose flour. Continue kneading till dough is rather stiff, but smooth. This will take about 8 minutes. (To be sure you've kneaded long enough, set a timer for 8 minutes.)

8 Divide the bread dough in half. Shape each half into a smooth ball. Cover the balls of dough with a cloth. Let the dough rest for 10 minutes.

9 While dough is resting, grease an 8x4x2-inch loaf pan by putting a little bit of shortening on a folded paper towel. Spread the shortening evenly over the bottom and the sides of the pan. After the dough has rested 10 minutes, use your hands to roll each ball of dough into a 12-inch-long rope.

(CONTINUED on next page)

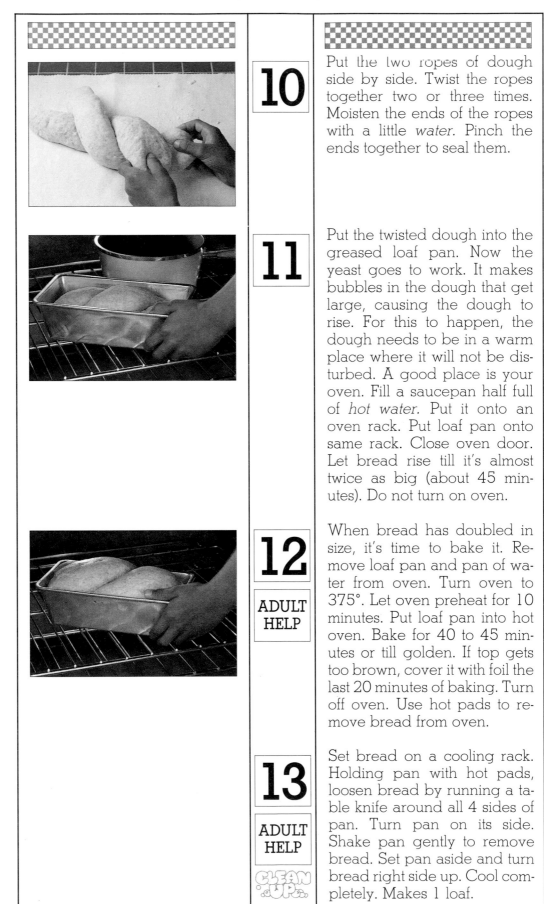

10 Put the two ropes of dough side by side. Twist the ropes together two or three times. Moisten the ends of the ropes with a little *water*. Pinch the ends together to seal them.

11 Put the twisted dough into the greased loaf pan. Now the yeast goes to work. It makes bubbles in the dough that get large, causing the dough to rise. For this to happen, the dough needs to be in a warm place where it will not be disturbed. A good place is your oven. Fill a saucepan half full of *hot water*. Put it onto an oven rack. Put loaf pan onto same rack. Close oven door. Let bread rise till it's almost twice as big (about 45 minutes). Do not turn on oven.

12 ADULT HELP When bread has doubled in size, it's time to bake it. Remove loaf pan and pan of water from oven. Turn oven to 375°. Let oven preheat for 10 minutes. Put loaf pan into hot oven. Bake for 40 to 45 minutes or till golden. If top gets too brown, cover it with foil the last 20 minutes of baking. Turn off oven. Use hot pads to remove bread from oven.

13 ADULT HELP CLEAN UP Set bread on a cooling rack. Holding pan with hot pads, loosen bread by running a table knife around all 4 sides of pan. Turn pan on its side. Shake pan gently to remove bread. Set pan aside and turn bread right side up. Cool completely. Makes 1 loaf.

1

WASH HANDS

ADULT HELP

Measure water. Put water into a 3-quart saucepan. Put pan onto burner. Turn burner to high heat. When water starts to boil, add spaghetti a little at a time. (If you add it all at once, the water will stop boiling.) After you've added all the spaghetti, cook for 10 to 12 minutes or just till tender. To see if it is done, use a fork to remove a piece of spaghetti from pan. Rinse under cold water, then taste to see if it's tender. If it's still chewy, cook for 2 to 3 minutes more and test again. Turn off burner.

2

ADULT HELP

To drain the spaghetti, put a colander into the sink. Carefully pour spaghetti out of the saucepan into colander. (Be very careful because steam will rise out of the sink and can be very hot.)

3

Let spaghetti stand for a few minutes to drain well. Put into a large mixing bowl. Measure butter or margarine. Use a rubber scraper to stir butter into hot spaghetti till butter melts.

4

Crack one of the eggs on the side of a small bowl. Working over the bowl, gently separate the eggshell halves and pour the egg into the bowl. Repeat with second egg. Use the fork to beat eggs lightly till yolks and whites of the eggs are mixed well. Measure Parmesan cheese. Use a fork to stir cheese into eggs. Pour egg-cheese mixture over spaghetti in bowl. Use the rubber scraper to stir till mixed well.

(CONTINUED on next page)

EQUIPMENT

range top
oven
measuring cups
3-quart saucepan
fork
colander
large mixing bowl
rubber scraper
small bowl
9-inch pie plate
paper towel
spoon
cutting board
sharp knife
wooden spoon
long-handled spoon
can *or* container for grease
can opener
hot pads

INGREDIENTS

6 cups water
6 ounces spaghetti
2 tablespoons butter *or* margarine
2 eggs
⅓ cup grated Parmesan cheese
Shortening
½ pound ground beef
1 medium onion
1 8-ounce can pizza sauce
1 1½-ounce slice mozzarella *or* cheddar cheese

5 Grease a 9-inch pie plate by putting a little bit of shortening on a folded paper towel. Then spread the shortening evenly over bottom and sides of pie plate. Pour the spaghetti mixture into the greased pie plate. Press spaghetti with the back of a spoon to form it into a crust, building up the sides.

6 ADULT HELP Turn oven to 350°. Use your hands to break up the ground beef as you put it into the same 3-quart pan you cooked the spaghetti in. To chop the onion, on a cutting board use a sharp knife to peel onion; cut in half. Cut halves into several slices; cut across slices to make small pieces. Add chopped onion to ground beef. Put pan onto burner. Turn burner to medium-high heat. Cook and stir with a wooden spoon till no pink color is left in meat.

7 ADULT HELP Turn off burner. Take pan off burner. Use a long-handled spoon to push the ground beef to one side of the pan. Tip the pan a little bit so the grease runs to the other side. Use the spoon to very carefully put the grease into a can or container an adult gives you.

8 Use a can opener to open the can of pizza sauce. Use the rubber scraper to empty the sauce into the ground beef mixture. Stir till mixed well. Spoon meat mixture into the spaghetti crust. Use the back of the spoon to spread mixture evenly over bottom of crust.

Put the pie into hot oven. Bake for 20 minutes. (**A**) While the pie is baking, on the cutting board use the sharp knife to cut the cheese slice twice to make 3 rectangles. (**B**) Cut each rectangle from corner to corner to make 2 triangles. You will have 6 triangles of cheese.

Use hot pads to remove pie from oven. Arrange cheese triangles on top of pie. Use hot pads to put pie back into oven. Bake about 5 minutes more or till cheese is just melted. Turn off oven. Use hot pads to remove pie from oven. Let pie stand for 5 minutes before serving. Makes 6 servings.

9
ADULT HELP

10
ADULT HELP

CLEAN UP

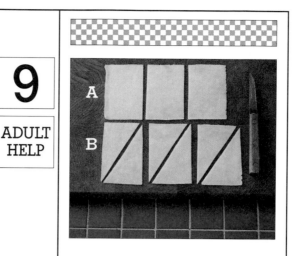

TRY IT THIS WAY

Deluxe Spaghetti-Crust Pie: Follow the recipe for the *Spaghetti-Crust Pie, but* spread 1 cup *cream-style cottage cheese* over the spaghetti crust. Then spread the ground beef mixture over the cottage cheese.

PIZZA PORK CHOPS

EQUIPMENT

range top
oven
measuring cups
  and spoons
cutting board
sharp knife
medium sauce-
  pan
wooden spoon
kitchen scissors
12x7½x2-inch
  baking dish
can opener
strainer
small bowl
foil
tongs
fork
hot pads
pancake turner

INGREDIENTS

4 pork chops, cut
  ¾ inch thick
3 tablespoons
  butter *or*
  margarine
1 small onion
1 8-ounce package
  (2 cups) herb-
  seasoned
  stuffing mix
½ cup water
¼ teaspoon dried
  oregano
1 8-ounce can
  pizza sauce
1 3-ounce can
  sliced
  mushrooms
1 4-ounce package
  (1 cup) shred-
  ded mozzarella
  cheese

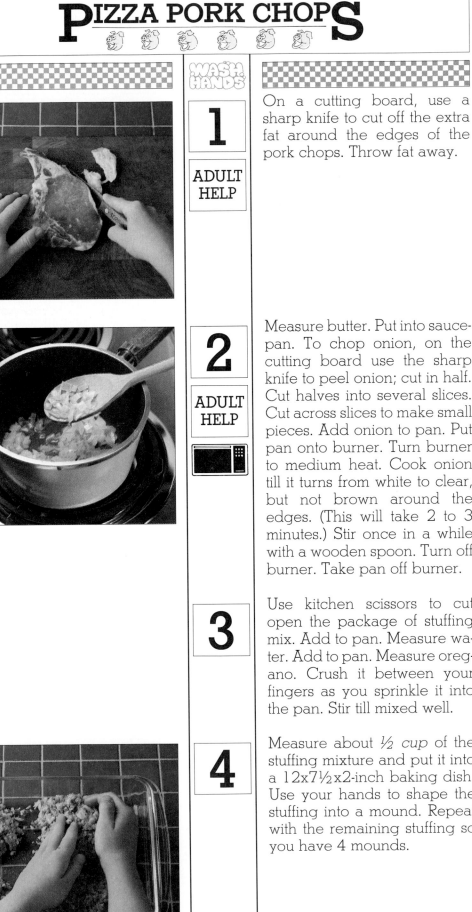

1

ADULT HELP

On a cutting board, use a sharp knife to cut off the extra fat around the edges of the pork chops. Throw fat away.

2

ADULT HELP

Measure butter. Put into sauce-pan. To chop onion, on the cutting board use the sharp knife to peel onion; cut in half. Cut halves into several slices. Cut across slices to make small pieces. Add onion to pan. Put pan onto burner. Turn burner to medium heat. Cook onion till it turns from white to clear, but not brown around the edges. (This will take 2 to 3 minutes.) Stir once in a while with a wooden spoon. Turn off burner. Take pan off burner.

3

Use kitchen scissors to cut open the package of stuffing mix. Add to pan. Measure water. Add to pan. Measure oreg-ano. Crush it between your fingers as you sprinkle it into the pan. Stir till mixed well.

4

Measure about *½ cup* of the stuffing mixture and put it into a 12x7½x2-inch baking dish. Use your hands to shape the stuffing into a mound. Repeat with the remaining stuffing so you have 4 mounds.

Plenty of cheese on these pork chops makes them
extra-specially yummy!

85

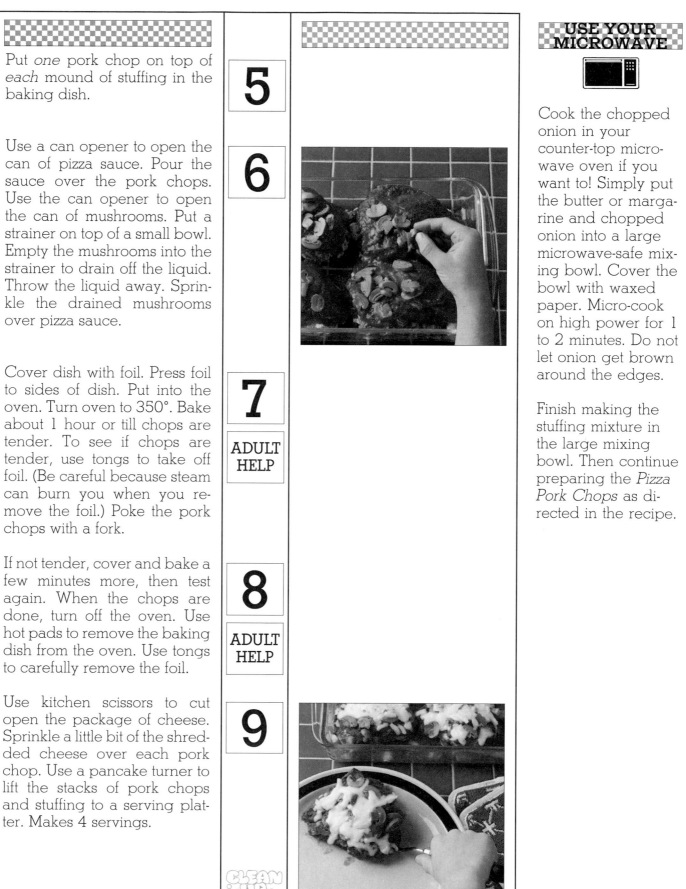

Put *one* pork chop on top of *each* mound of stuffing in the baking dish.

5

6

Use a can opener to open the can of pizza sauce. Pour the sauce over the pork chops. Use the can opener to open the can of mushrooms. Put a strainer on top of a small bowl. Empty the mushrooms into the strainer to drain off the liquid. Throw the liquid away. Sprinkle the drained mushrooms over pizza sauce.

Cover dish with foil. Press foil to sides of dish. Put into the oven. Turn oven to 350°. Bake about 1 hour or till chops are tender. To see if chops are tender, use tongs to take off foil. (Be careful because steam can burn you when you remove the foil.) Poke the pork chops with a fork.

7

ADULT HELP

If not tender, cover and bake a few minutes more, then test again. When the chops are done, turn off the oven. Use hot pads to remove the baking dish from the oven. Use tongs to carefully remove the foil.

8

ADULT HELP

Use kitchen scissors to cut open the package of cheese. Sprinkle a little bit of the shredded cheese over each pork chop. Use a pancake turner to lift the stacks of pork chops and stuffing to a serving platter. Makes 4 servings.

9

CLEAN UP

USE YOUR MICROWAVE

Cook the chopped onion in your counter-top microwave oven if you want to! Simply put the butter or margarine and chopped onion into a large microwave-safe mixing bowl. Cover the bowl with waxed paper. Micro-cook on high power for 1 to 2 minutes. Do not let onion get brown around the edges.

Finish making the stuffing mixture in the large mixing bowl. Then continue preparing the *Pizza Pork Chops* as directed in the recipe.

CHUNKY CHOCOLATE COOKIES

EQUIPMENT

oven
measuring cups
 and spoons
mixing bowl
wooden spoon
large mixer bowl
electric mixer
rubber scraper
small bowl
2 cookie sheets
2 small spoons
hot pads
pancake turner
cooling rack

INGREDIENTS

½ cup butter *or*
 margarine
1¼ cups all-purpose
 flour
½ teaspoon baking
 soda
½ cup packed
 brown sugar
¼ cup sugar
1 egg
1½ teaspoons vanilla
6 1.45-ounce bars
 milk chocolate

WASH HANDS

1 Soften the butter or margarine by setting it out of the refrigerator at least 30 minutes before making the cookies. This will make it easy to mix. When you're ready to make the cookies, turn oven to 375°. Measure flour and baking soda. Put them into a mixing bowl. Use a wooden spoon to stir the flour and soda together till mixed well. Set the flour mixture aside.

2 **ADULT HELP** Put the softened butter or margarine into a large mixer bowl. Turn an electric mixer to medium speed and beat the butter or margarine for 30 seconds. Turn off mixer. Measure the brown sugar and sugar. Add to the mixer bowl. Turn mixer to medium speed and beat about 1 minute or till mixed well. Turn off mixer. Use a rubber scraper to scrape sides of mixer bowl and beaters.

3 **ADULT HELP** Crack the egg on the side of the small bowl. Working over the bowl, gently separate the eggshell halves. Pour egg into small bowl. Add egg to the mixer bowl. Measure the vanilla. Add it to mixer bowl. Turn electric mixer to medium speed. Beat for 1 minute or till mixed well. Turn off mixer. Use rubber scraper to scrape sides of bowl and beaters.

4 **ADULT HELP** Pour about *half* of the flour mixture into mixer bowl. Turn the electric mixer to low speed and beat to mix in the flour. Turn off mixer. Add the rest of the flour mixture. Turn the mixer to low speed and beat till mixed well. Turn off mixer.

A "chunk of chocolate" waits for you in every bite of these kid favorites!

87

5

ADULT HELP

Use your fingers to break unwrapped chocolate bars into small pieces. Put the pieces of chocolate into the mixer bowl. Turn the electric mixer to low speed and beat the chocolate pieces into the cookie dough. Turn off the mixer.

6

To drop the dough onto the cookie sheet, get enough dough on a small spoon so the dough is slightly humped in the spoon. With the back of another small spoon, push the dough onto one of the cookie sheets. Leave about 2 inches between each cookie.

7

ADULT HELP

Put the cookie sheet into the hot oven. Bake the cookies for 8 to 10 minutes or till the cookies are golden brown. Meanwhile, drop some more cookie dough the same way onto the other cookie sheet.

8

ADULT HELP

Use hot pads to remove the cookie sheet from the oven. Put the second sheet of cookies into the oven. Let the baked cookies cool for 1 minute on the cookie sheet. Use a pancake turner to lift cookies onto a cooling rack. When the first cookie sheet is cool, drop more dough onto it. Bake the rest of the cookies the same way. Turn off the oven. Makes about 48 cookies.

CLEAN UP

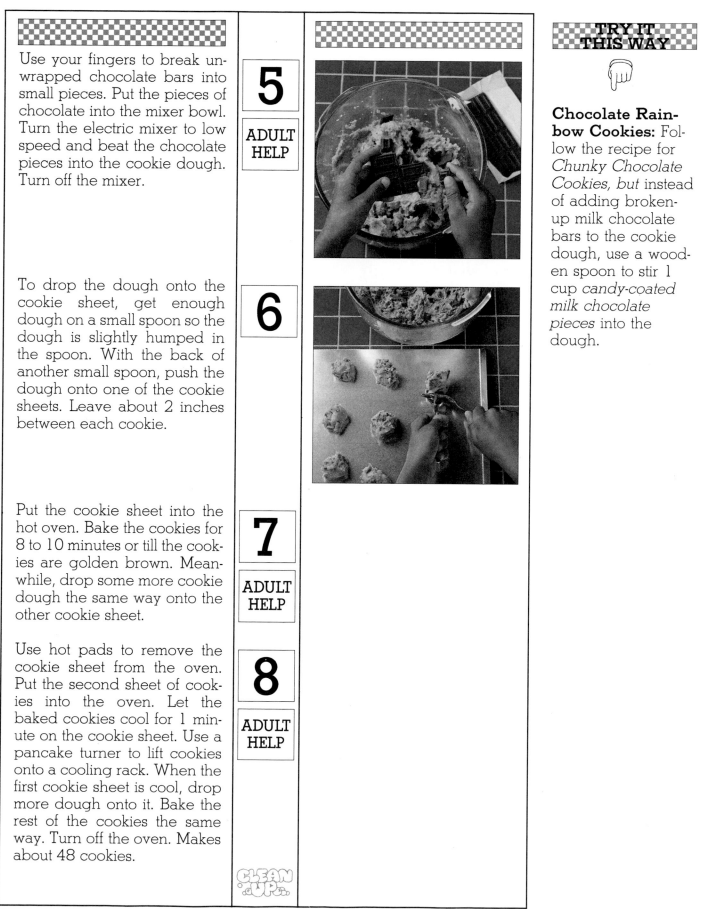

TRY IT THIS WAY

Chocolate Rainbow Cookies: Follow the recipe for *Chunky Chocolate Cookies,* but instead of adding broken-up milk chocolate bars to the cookie dough, use a wooden spoon to stir 1 cup *candy-coated milk chocolate pieces* into the dough.

CHERRY-BERRY JAM

EQUIPMENT

range top
measuring cups
bowl
large mixing
  bowl
potato masher
cutting board
sharp knife
rubber scraper
1½-quart sauce-
  pan
wooden spoon
ladle
5 or 6 half-pint
  jars with lids
  or freezer con-
  tainers with lids
ruler
wide-mouth
  funnel
damp cloth

INGREDIENTS

3 cups frozen
    pitted dark
    sweet cherries
2 cups frozen
    whole unsweet-
    ened *or* fresh
    strawberries
4¼ cups sugar
¾ cup water
1 1¾-ounce
    package
    powdered fruit
    pectin

1 Measure frozen cherries; put into a bowl. Measure frozen strawberries; put into a large mixing bowl. Let stand for 30 minutes to thaw. (If using fresh strawberries, rinse under cold running water; drain well. Use your fingers to pull stems off berries; put into large mixing bowl.)

2 Use a potato masher to mash the thawed or fresh strawberries till they're almost smooth.

3 ADULT HELP On a cutting board, use a sharp knife to cut the thawed cherries into small pieces. Put the cherry pieces into the bowl with mashed strawberries. If any liquid came out of cherries as they were thawing, add this liquid to bowl with strawberries and cherries.

4 Measure sugar. Add sugar to large mixing bowl. Use a rubber scraper to stir till mixed well. Let stand for 10 minutes.

5 ADULT HELP While the mixture is standing, measure the water. Pour the water into a 1½-quart saucepan. Use a wooden spoon to stir the pectin into the water in the pan. Put the pan onto burner. Turn burner to high heat. Cook the pectin-water mixture till it comes to a full rolling boil. (A full rolling boil is a boil that does not stop even if you stir it.) The mixture should be boiling over the whole surface.

After the pectin-water mixture comes to a full rolling boil, continue to cook it for 1 minute, stirring all the time with the wooden spoon. (It's a good idea to set a timer for 1 minute so you know exactly how long to let the mixture boil.) After boiling and stirring for 1 minute, turn off burner. Take the pan off the burner.

6 ADULT HELP

Very carefully pour the hot pectin-water mixture over the fruit mixture in the large bowl. Use the wooden spoon to stir for 3 minutes. (You could set your timer for 3 minutes.)

7 ADULT HELP

Use a ladle to very carefully put the jam into clean half-pint jars or freezer containers. Ladle the hot jam into the jars or freezer containers, filling each to within ½ inch of the top. To make it easier to ladle jam into jars, first put a wide-mouth funnel in the jar opening.

8 ADULT HELP

After the jars or freezer containers are filled, use a damp cloth to wipe off any jam that may have gotten on the rims of the jars or freezer containers. Cover jars or freezer containers with lids. Close tightly.

9

Let the jam stand at room temperature for several hours or till set. Store jam in the refrigerator for up to 3 weeks or in the freezer for up to 3 months. Makes 5 or 6 half-pints.

10

CLEAN UP

TRY IT THIS WAY

Peach-Berry Jam: Follow the recipe for *Cherry-Berry Jam, but* use 3 cups *frozen peach slices* instead of the frozen cherries. Thaw the peaches and save the liquid. Cut the thawed peaches into small pieces. Put the peaches and the liquid into the large mixing bowl with the mashed strawberries. Continue as directed in the recipe.

WHAT DO YOU KNOW?

It is a good idea to label your jam by writing the date and the kind of jam on a piece of paper and fastening the paper to the jar. Then the information will be handy when you need it. You will not have to guess what kind of jam is in the jar or how long you should keep it.

Cake Decorating

Begin with a cake that has been baked in a 13x9x2-inch baking pan. It must be completely cool before you begin.

Add 1 or 2 drops of *blue food coloring* to one 16.5-ounce can *creamy white frosting*. Use a spoon to stir food coloring into frosting till it is mixed well. Using a narrow metal spatula or table knife, spread the colored frosting over top of cake.

Using a squeeze tube of *yellow decorator icing* and a petal tip, make the ribbons on the cake. Make each ribbon about 1½ inches wide. Have one ribbon run lengthwise on the cake and one crosswise on the cake. (Practice squeezing the tube of decorator icing on waxed paper before you begin.)

Use a squeeze tube of *white decorator icing* and a writing tip to outline the yellow frosting ribbons.

On a cutting board, use a sharp knife to cut 1 large *lemon* in half, cutting from top to bottom. Cut each half into 3 wedges. Arrange the lemon wedges on the cake where the 2 ribbons meet so they look like a bow!

If you like, use a squeeze tube of *decorator icing* and a writing tip to write a name or a message on the frosted cake. Wouldn't somebody you know be pleased to have a cake decorated by you?

MENU
SUNDAY DINNER

Crispy Oven Chicken

Baked Potatoes

Tomato Wedges
on Lettuce

Peanut Butter-Peach
Crisp

Milk or iced tea

Sunday dinner is a time when the whole family sits down together to eat; so what better opportunity to show off your cooking talents!

Before you begin, read through the following three pages to make sure you understand everything. Check the ingredient and equipment lists in the recipes to be sure you have everything you need. (This menu will feed four people.)

This dinner is special because all three hot dishes cook in the oven at the same time. First, put the oven racks on the bottom shelf position and the top shelf position of your oven. Then, begin preparing the dinner.

When setting the table, you'll need a glass, fork, knife, spoon, and napkin for each person. Also, keep the dinner plates in the kitchen so you can arrange the salads on them. Keep the dessert plates in the kitchen so they'll be handy when it's time to serve the dessert.

When dinner is all ready to eat, sit down, relax, and enjoy!

Get Ready for Dinner

- **1½ hours before serving:** To prepare Baked Potatoes, scrub 4 baking potatoes with a vegetable brush. Remove any sprouts. Use a fork to prick potatoes in several places. Put potatoes along sides of top oven rack. Turn oven to 375°. Bake for 1½ hours. When potatoes are done baking, cut an X through each potato, making a small opening. Put butter into opening. If you like, add dairy sour cream; sprinkle with cooked bacon pieces.

- **1 hour and 20 minutes before serving:** Prepare the **CRISPY OVEN CHICKEN.** Follow recipe directions at right.

- **1 hour before serving:** Put chicken on bottom oven rack. Prepare the **PEANUT BUTTER-PEACH CRISP.** Follow recipe directions on next page. Set dessert aside. Set the table.

- **20 minutes before serving:** Put the **PEANUT BUTTER-PEACH CRISP** on top oven rack. To prepare Tomato Wedges on Lettuce, rinse 2 large tomatoes and 4 small lettuce leaves in cold water. Pat dry. On a cutting board, use a sharp knife to cut each tomato into 6 wedges. Put 1 lettuce leaf on each dinner plate. Arrange 3 tomato wedges on each lettuce leaf. Place dinner plates on the table.

- **At serving time:** Pour milk or iced tea. Remove the **CRISPY OVEN CHICKEN,** Baked Potatoes, and the **PEANUT BUTTER-PEACH CRISP** from oven. Put the chicken and potatoes onto platters; set on table. Let **PEANUT BUTTER-PEACH CRISP** stand while you eat dinner. Serve with ice cream.

CRISPY OVEN CHICKEN

EQUIPMENT

range top
oven
measuring spoons
plastic bag
rolling pin
pie plate
small saucepan
wooden spoon
paper towels
waxed paper
pastry brush
13x9x2-inch baking pan
fork
hot pads
tongs

INGREDIENTS

1 3-ounce can chow mein noodles
2 tablespoons butter *or* margarine
2 tablespoons honey
1 tablespoon lemon juice
2 teaspoons soy sauce
8 chicken drumsticks *or* thighs

 Put the chow mein noodles into a plastic bag. Close the bag. Use a rolling pin to crush the noodles. Pour the crushed chow mein noodles into a pie plate.

 ADULT HELP Measure butter or margarine. Put butter or margarine into a small saucepan. Put saucepan onto burner. Turn burner to low heat. When butter or margarine melts, turn off burner. Take saucepan off burner. Measure the honey, lemon juice, and soy sauce. Add to saucepan with melted butter or margarine. Use a wooden spoon to stir till mixed well.

 Rinse the chicken under cold water. Pat dry with paper towels. Put chicken pieces onto waxed paper. Using a pastry brush, brush the chicken pieces on all sides with butter-honey mixture. Roll each chicken piece in the crushed chow mein noodles till coated. Put the chicken pieces into a 13x9x2-inch baking pan. Sprinkle any extra crushed chow mein noodles over the chicken pieces.

 ADULT HELP Put the baking pan into the hot 375° oven on the bottom oven rack. Bake about 1 hour or till chicken is tender. To see if chicken is tender, poke the pieces with a fork. Turn off oven. Use hot pads to remove pan from oven. Use tongs to place chicken on a serving platter. Makes 4 servings.

SUNDAY
DINNER MENU
(continued)

PEANUT BUTTER-PEACH CRISP

EQUIPMENT

oven
measuring spoons
can opener
strainer
bowl
1-quart casserole
mixing bowl
fork
hot pads

INGREDIENTS

1 16-ounce can
   peach or pear
   slices
3 tablespoons all-
   purpose flour
3 tablespoons
   brown sugar
3 tablespoons
   quick-cooking
   rolled oats
1/8 teaspoon ground
   cinnamon
2 tablespoons
   creamy peanut
   butter
1 tablespoon
   butter or
   margarine
   Vanilla ice
   cream

 Use a can opener to open the can of peaches or pears. Put a strainer on top of a bowl. Empty the peaches or pears into the strainer to drain. (Save the peach or pear liquid to use another time.) Put the drained peaches or pears into a 1-quart casserole.

 Measure the flour, brown sugar, rolled oats, and cinnamon. Put them into a mixing bowl. Use a fork to stir till mixed well. Measure the peanut butter and butter or margarine. Put them into the bowl with the flour mixture. Use the fork to mix the peanut butter and butter or margarine into the flour mixture till it is crumbly. Use your fingers to sprinkle the crumb mixture over the peaches or pears in the 1-quart casserole.

 Put the casserole into the hot 375° oven on the top oven rack. Bake for 20 minutes. Turn off oven. Use hot pads to remove the casserole from the oven. Serve the crisp warm with vanilla ice cream. Makes 4 to 6 servings.